# Romania

# Romania

BY TERRI WILLIS

*Enchantment of the World*
*Second Series*

Children's Press®

*A Division of Grolier Publishing*

NEW YORK   LONDON   HONG KONG   SYDNEY
DANBURY, CONNECTICUT

**Frontispiece:** Village architecture in Romania

*Consultant:* Tatyana Nestorova, Ph.D., Lecturer, Undergraduate International Studies Program, The Ohio State University

*Please note: All statistics are as up-to-date as possible at the time of publication.*

Visit Children's Press on the Internet: http://publishing.grolier.com

Book Production by Herman Adler Design

Library of Congress Cataloging-in-Publication Data

Willis, Terri.
    Romania / by Terri Willis.
       p. cm. — (Enchantment of the world. Second series)
    Includes bibliographical references and index.
    Summary: Describes the geography, history, plants and animals, economy, language, religions, culture, and people of Romania.
    ISBN 0-516-21635-X
    1. Romania—Juvenile literature. [1. Romania.] I. Title. II. Series.
DR205.W55  2000
949.8—dc21

99-37403
CIP

# Romania

# Contents

**Cover photo:**
A boy in the
Carpathian
Mountains wearing
a traditional fur hat

**CHAPTER**

A mountain lake

A terracotta statue

# Inspiration from the Past, Hope for the Future

Romania today occupies precisely 91,699 square miles (237,482 square kilometers) in eastern Europe. But it has not always been this size or had the same boundaries. Over the centuries, Romania has been larger and it has been smaller. Its borders have been changed by wars and by treaties. Much blood and many tears have been shed along the way. It seems almost always to have been a region of conflict.

This may be due to Romania's location on the edge of eastern Europe in the region known as the Balkans. Historically, the region has been crossed over and fought over, and to dominate Romania was to have a foothold in this influential part of the world. Romania is a land of fertile soil, great mineral deposits, and access to the important Danube River and Black Sea. Because of these resources, dominating Romania meant economic strength.

*Opposite:* **Medieval buildings in Sighisoara**

**The Olt River flows into the Danube River.**

Each foreign oppressor and each corrupt ruler brought its own brand of trouble to the Romanian people. But they endured. Armies of Romanian peasants banded together to fight for freedom. Artists risked their lives to tell the truth about their nation's struggles. Philosophers and activists appealed to the rest of the world for help. Some rulers brought hope, while others only increased the pain of the Romanian people.

The reasons for Romania's tumultuous past are many. Each war had its own purpose and each ruler had his own agenda. Sometimes trouble came from within. For example, the corrupt leader Nicolae Ceaușescu brought enormous

A protester holds up a burning image of Nicolae Ceaușescu.

misery to his fellow Romanians during the twenty-four years he headed the nation. Though it has been more than a decade since 1989, when he was killed in a revolution of the Romanian people, the country is still trying to undo the damage he caused.

Under Ceauşescu, the strength and the spirit of the Romanian people were challenged once again. And still their strength and spirit remained intact.

## A Nation Set Apart

The Balkans are a group of republics and countries in southeastern Europe, named for a mountain range in the area. The Balkans include Slovenia, Croatia, Bosnia and Herzegovina, Macedonia, Serbia, Albania, Greece, Bulgaria, Turkey (most of which is Asia), and Romania. While history has long grouped the Balkan nations together, Romania stands apart. Like most of the Balkans, it emerged from communist rule toward the end of the twentieth century. But while many Balkan nations remain bogged down by serious ethnic conflicts, Romania is trying hard to remain peaceful, to advance its economy, and to build positive relationships with Western nations.

Native Romanians view themselves as one of the world's Latin cultures. This is because many Romanian people are descended from the Romans, who occupied the country from A.D. 106 to A.D. 271. Other Romanians are descended from the Dacians, who inhabited Romania earlier, and from the tribes of Huns, Goths, and Slavs who controlled the region

Geopolitical map of
Romania

**ROMANIA**

- Cities of over 100,000 people
- ○ Smaller cities and towns

| 0 | 200 miles |
| 0 | 300 kilometers |

SLOVAKIA

UKRAINE

Romania

MOLDOVA

HUNGARY

Satu Mare

Baia Mare    *BUKOVINA*

Paşcani    Iaşi

*Bistriţa*    Roman

Oradea    Cluj-Napoca

Tinca    Bacău

Tîrgu Mureş    *MOLDAVIA*

Arad    Brad    Mediaş

Timişoara    *Mureş*    Sibiu    Focşani

Braşov    Galaţi
Brăila

*BANAT*    *TRANSYLVANIA*

Oraviţa    Buzău

Orşova    Piteşti    Ialomtja    Ploieşti

*Jiu*    *Olt*    *DOBROGEA*

*Danube*    *Argeş*

Iron Gate    *WALACHIA*    ☆ Bucharest    Constanţa
Dam    Craiova

SERBIA    Caracal    *Danube*

Black
Sea

*N*

*W*    *E*    BULGARIA

*S*

MACEDONIA    TURKEY

GREECE

later. But it was from the Romans that Romanians drew their name, and it is from Romans that they draw their identity, too.

Romania has given the world fine athletes, including Olympic gymnast Nadia Comaneci. They also have a tradition of great art, music, and literature from the most remote mountain village to large urban centers. "If only our administration and politics were on the same level as the arts, we would be one of the happiest countries on earth," said Georges Enesco, a famous Romanian composer and violinist.

The Romanian people have held on to their traditions and have found strength in remembering the valiant struggles of those before them. As each successive generation steadies itself to move forward in the world, it seems to find inspiration in the past and hope in the future.

Gymnast Nadia Comaneci performing in the 1976 Olympics, where she won three gold medals

Children from the region of Moldavia

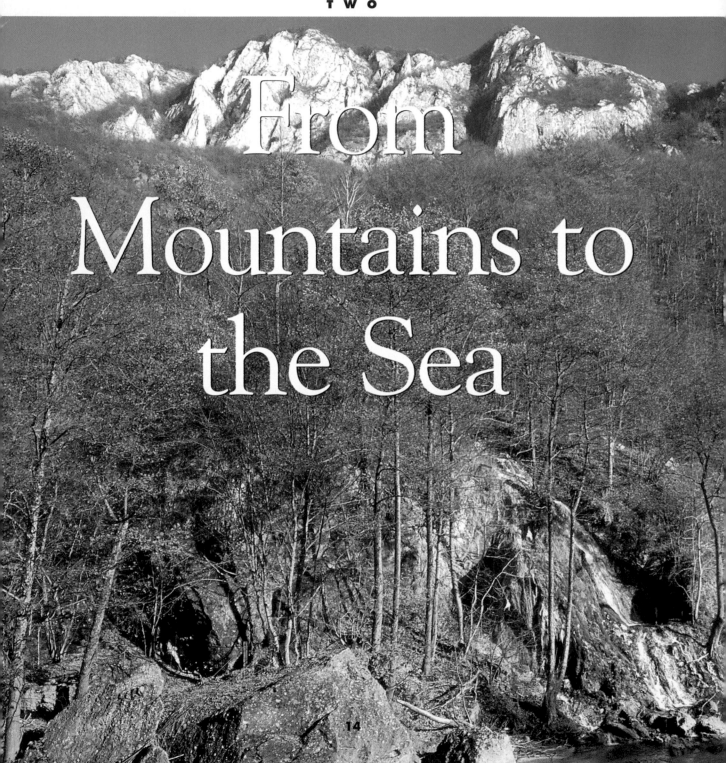

# From Mountains to the Sea

14

**R**OMANIA IS LOCATED HALFWAY BETWEEN THE EQUATOR and the North Pole and midway between Europe's eastern-most and westernmost points. It is slightly smaller than the state of Oregon.

Romania's neighbor to the north is Ukraine, and its north-western boundary lies along the nation of Hungary. The Danube River forms part of the border between Romania and Serbia to the southwest and Bulgaria to the south. To the east, the Prut River forms a natural boundary with Moldova.

Romania's topography, or physical features, can almost be broken down into thirds. Mountains, mostly undeveloped and covered with trees, make up 31 percent. Uplands—hills and high plateaus broken up by small farming communities and villages—cover 33 percent of the land. And 36 percent consists of plains, where agriculture, industry, and big cities dominate. These statistics, however, don't describe the beauty, grandeur, and magnificent diversity of Romania's landscape.

*Opposite:* **Transylvania's Aries River**

**A mountain waterfall**

## Romania's Geographical Features

**Highest Elevation:**
Mount Moldoveanu,
8,343 feet (2,543 m)
above sea level

**Lowest Elevation:**
Sea level, along the
Black Sea coast

**Largest City:** Bucharest,
population 2.4 million

**Longest River:**
The Danube, flowing
668 miles (1,075 km)
through Romania,
mostly along the
southern border

**Highest Temperature
Recorded:** 111° F (44° C)
in the southern plains

**Lowest Temperature
Recorded:** -36° F (-38° C)
in the Transylvanian Alps near Braşov

**Largest Lake:** Razelm, near the Danube Delta, 160 square miles (415 sq km)

**Area:** 91,699 square miles (237,482 sq km)

**Greatest Distance:** 450 miles (724 km) east to west

POLAND

SLOVAKIA

UKRAINE

HUNGARY

MOLDOVA

Someş
Oradea
BIHOR MTNS.
Cluj-Napoca
Mureş
Timişoara
Sibiu
Peleaga
Olt
Orşova
Craiova

CARPATHIANS
Paşcani
Bistriţa
Bicaz Gorge
Prut
Iaşi
Siret
Moldoveanu
TRANSYLVANIAN ALPS
Galaţi
Brăila
Bucharest
Brăila
Marshes
Delta of the Danube
Danube
Constanţa

SERBIA

BALKAN MTNS.

BULGARIA

Black
Sea

0    100 miles
0    150 km

## Romania's Regions

There are three major regions in Romania—Transylvania,
Moldavia, and Walachia—and three smaller regions—
Banat, Bukovina, and Dobrogea. These regions have no real

governmental importance anymore—they are not recognized with official boundaries and jurisdictions. But to the people who live in them, the regions play a primary role in how they view themselves and their homes. Each has its own traditions and history, heavily influenced by its unique geography.

## *Transylvania*

Transylvania includes much of Romania's Carpathian Mountains, which offer some of the country's most outstanding scenery. The Carpathians, created during Earth's Tertiary Period, are more than 25 million years old. They curve around

**A lake in the Carpathian Mountains**

the eastern and southern edges of Transylvania. The Transylvanian Alps are actually the southern range of the Carpathians, and the highest range as well. Romania's highest point, Mount Moldoveanu, which reaches to 8,343 feet (2,543 meters), is in the Carpathians. Nearby is Mount Negoiu at 8,317 feet (2,535 m). In Romania, mountain peaks at this altitude are always covered in ice and snow.

Glaciers helped to shape the Carpathian Mountains, and there is still evidence of them today. Cirques (serks) are one example. These steep-sided hollows were formed when the waters from melting glaciers carried away the soil, cutting deep grooves into the land. Cirques are found along many valleys in the Alps. The last Ice Age also left behind many beautiful glacial lakes surrounded by heavily forested slopes.

Most of the Northern Carpathian Mountains are composed of volcanic rock, granite, and hard crystalline, giving them a jagged, imposing appearance. But the southern Carpathians are made of limestone and sandstone, eroded over the years by wind and water. These mountains have unusual shapes, and rivers winding through their gorges etch weird formations in the rock.

### Romanian Ski Resorts

Many skiers rate the resorts in the Carpathian Mountains among the best in Europe. Most were built in the 1960s and 1970s, with cable ski lifts and several runs ranging from easy to very difficult. Some runs are up to 12,467 feet (3,800 m) long. The ski season runs from December through March, but the resorts are in use year-round. In the early summer, the mountains are alive with wildflowers, and the ski lifts carry hikers to the higher altitudes. The resorts play host to many people who enjoy the bounty of mountain wildlife. Fishing, bird-watching, and camping are popular activities.

There are spectacular caves in the Transylvanian Alps.

The spectacular caves found in the Transylvanian Alps are another effect of erosion over many centuries. Underground water percolates up to the surface through limestone, creating huge, intricate caverns and underground rivers that flow for miles before reaching the surface.

Some of the country's largest caves are found in the western Carpathians. This is where Romania's earliest inhabitants lived, during the Stone Age. These mountains, the lowest in Romania, are not a continuous range. Instead, they are made up of clusters of mountains separated by deep valleys, sometimes called "gates." Throughout history, invaders from the east gained access to the lands of what is now Romania through these gates.

**Braşov is in the foothills of the Transylvanian Alps.**

Transylvania is one of Romania's most prosperous regions. Its interior is a plateau of rolling foothills and quiet villages with an average altitude of about 1,500 feet (457 m). This important agricultural region also has large underground deposits of salt and natural gas. The natural gas reserves, first located about seventy years ago, are the region's most valuable resource. The salt is mined, and it also adds to the area's salt lakes, which attract tourists.

## Moldavia

Most of Romania east of Transylvania is the region of Moldavia. It is bordered on the west by the Carpathian Mountains and on the east by the Prut River. The land is mostly plateau—sheer cliffs towering over narrow valleys.

**Farmland in Moldavia**

## The Accursed River

The Prut River forms Romania's eastern border with the countries of Moldova and Ukraine. For years, the Prut was known to locals as the *riu blastemat* (accursed river), because many of ancient Romania's invaders made their way into the country across this watery passageway, leaving behind a trail of blood.

Galaţi is a city at the southernmost tip of the Prut River in Moldavia. Near here, the Prut River meets the Danube. The Siretul River also flows southward through Moldavia and enters the Danube near Galaţi, making Galaţi a major river port. Another river flowing through Moldavia is the Bistriţa River. Only about 15 feet (4.6 m) wide in most spots, the river

**A road winding through the Bicaz Gorge**

has cut a 1,000-foot (305-m)-deep gorge in the valley. This is the spectacular Bicaz Gorge, so deep that sunlight rarely reaches its floor.

Red Lake, in the Bistriţa Valley, reflects the color of the red granite mountains that surround it; hence its name. Some of the other hills in Moldavia contain sandy quartz. This mineral is quarried for use in the glass-making industry.

Farther north, in the eastern portion of Moldavia, grassy plains stretch along the border with Moldova. It is good land for farming, with rich black soil.

### Stephen the Great

Many streets in Romania are named for Ştefan cel Mare (Stephen the Great), a Moldavian prince who ruled from 1457 to 1504. He fought heroically against foreign invaders, especially the Ottoman Turks, in a struggle to keep his beloved Moldavia free. He defended Christianity in his homeland and wanted to keep out the Muslim faith of the Ottomans. Pope Sixtus IV named Stephen an "Athlete of Christ." Because of his great popularity, he was able to raise an army of 55,000 peasants. He won thirty-four of the thirty-six battles he fought, but ultimately, he was unable to unite other Christian nations to resist the Ottomans. On his deathbed, he advised his son, Bogdan the One-Eyed, to try to make an honorable peace treaty with the Ottomans.

Stephen the Great's tomb is in Putna Monastery. Stephen is buried there with his children and two wives, both named Maria. He built the monastery in 1466 and rebuilt it in 1480 after a fire.

For 500 years, streets have been named in his honor. He is remembered for his diligent defense of Moldavia and also as a great supporter of the arts and literature. Stephen the Great was responsible for building forty stone churches. He encouraged beauty to flourish throughout Moldavia.

## Walachia

Walachia (Va-LAH-hiah) is the major region of southern Romania, bordered by the Transylvanian Alps to the north and the Danube River to the south. Several rivers, including the Jiu, Argeş, and Ialomtja, run through Walachia to the Danube.

The southern part of the Danube River is more than 1 mile (1.6 km) wide. In spring, when the snow melts and rain falls, the resulting flooding makes the river even wider. On the low-lying Romanian side, the Danube spreads up to 10 miles (16 km) wide in places. When the floodwaters recede, the ground is prime for planting. This marshy land is an excellent place for growing crops, such as tomatoes and rice.

The rest of Walachia is mostly flat plains, formed by deposits left behind by glaciers and flowing water. This area has the country's best farmland, with rich soil called loess. Dams along the many rivers provide water for irrigation. Most of the nation's grain, particularly wheat and corn, is produced here. Sunflowers are also a plentiful crop.

## Banat

On the western edge of Romania, extending like a wedge between Transylvania and Walachia, is the region known as Banat. This land is mostly plains, and its fertile soil is good for farming. Wheat, barley, and corn are major crops. Coal and iron-ore are mined in the mountains to the south.

The Danube River separates Serbia (left) and Romania (right).

The Danube River enters Romania along its southwestern border with Serbia, through a series of narrow gorges called the Iron Gates. The strong current and large rocks of the Iron Gates make shipping difficult. Since 1896, the river has been partially tamed with a human-made channel and a series of locks and dams. Traces still remain

## Environmental Problems at the Iron Gates

Recent studies in the Black Sea area have turned up some serious environmental problems. The Iron Gates dam on the Danube River blocks the flow of silicates downriver—silicates in the water remain in the reservoir behind the dam.

Silicates are chemical compounds found in the rocks lining the river, and the river picks them up as it travels toward the Black Sea. These silicates are necessary for the growth of diatoms, which provide the food source for zooplankton. Zooplankton, in turn, are food for larger life forms in the sea. So the food chain in the Black Sea is being disrupted, and, in time, the sea's entire ecosystem may be changed. The Danube is suffering additional environmental problems as a result of NATO's 1999 conflict with Serbia. Several chemical plants in Belgrade, Serbia's capital, were bombed during the conflict, releasing harmful chemicals into the waterway less than 50 miles (80 km) upstream of the Romanian border. People were warned that eating fish from the river could be extremely dangerous to their health.

of stone bridges and roads built by the Romans nearly nineteen centuries ago. In 1971, Romania and Yugoslavia jointly completed a huge dam across the rapids, with a hydroelectric power station producing 2 million kilowatts of energy. Behind the dam, the waters of the Danube have formed an artificial lake, greatly improving navigation.

## Bukovina

Bukovina is one of Romania's smaller regions. It sometimes is not even considered a region on its own, but instead is grouped with Moldavia. It is a small, forested area on the eastern edge of the Northern Carpathian Mountains and home to many small villages.

### Looking at Romania's Cities

Constanța is a historic port city on the Black Sea in southeastern Romania. It has a population of about 350,000. As a trade center, it serves the local region as well as countries in the Mediterranean area. In the seventh century B.C., it was the site of a Greek city named Tomi. In 72 B.C., it came under Roman rule and was later renamed Constantiana in honor of Constantine I, Roman emperor from A.D. 306 to A.D. 337.

Iași (yash), located in Moldavia, is a cultural center with fine theaters, an orchestra, and important universities. It was founded in the 1560s by Moldavian princes. Today, Iași has about 340,000 residents.

Timișoara, in the Banat region, was originally a fortress for Hungarians dating back to the 1300s, and the city has been a political center in the area for centuries. It has about 328,000 residents, who enjoy its well-planned streets, many museums, and good restaurants.

## Black Sea Resorts

You thought baths were supposed to get the mud off your skin, right? Well, some people take baths *in* mud! In parts of Romania and elsewhere around the world, it is considered healthful to take baths in mud that contains special minerals. People travel for many miles to relax in the mud, particularly at resorts along the Black Sea, such as Eforie Nord, Eforie Sud, Neptun, and Mangalia. Some 160 spas are found throughout the country, one-third of all the mineral-water springs in Europe.

### Dobrogea

To the southeast of Moldavia is Dobrogea (DOH-bro-jah). It lies between the Danube River to the west and north, the Black Sea to east, and Bulgaria to the south. Bulgaria has controlled Dobrogea at various times throughout history. The central plateau of this region is at an altitude of about 820 feet (250 m) on average. Granite is quarried here.

Dobrogea's northeastern portion is mainly the vast Danube River Delta, a marshy land where the great river divides into three branches that flow into the sea. Land has formed between each of these channels as a result of the buildup of soil and debris washed down the Danube over centuries—about 70 million metric tons each year. This delta is a great habitat for wildlife.

## Hot Summers, Cold Winters

Though there is great diversity of landscape across Romania, the climate is fairly similar throughout the country. In general, the climate is humid-continental, with hot summers, cold winters, and an amount of precipitation—snow and rain—that remains fairly constant year-round.

Romania's climate is good for agriculture—the average summer temperature on the plains is 75° to 85° F (24° to 29° C). In winter, the average temperature in the capital, Bucharest, is 26° F (-3° C).

The few differences from area to area are caused by the mountains and the sea. For example, the air in the west is more humid because the Carpathian Mountains hold the moisture from the Atlantic Ocean in that part of the country. The mountains also keep the summer's hot, dry air from the south, and the winter's cold, dry air from the east, out of Transylvania. This means that there is more rainfall and snow in the mountains and plains of Transylvania than in other parts of Romania. Annual precipitation in the mountains can sometimes reach 50 inches (127 centimeters) or greater, more than twice the amount on the plains.

Along the Black Sea coastline, the large body of water helps to moderate temperatures, causing mild winters and warm—but not hot—summers. There is little precipitation along the coastline.

# Romania's Natural Riches

THE VARIED LANDSCAPE AND CLIMATIC CONDITIONS IN Romania provide just the right habitat for many plants and animals. From mountain forests to the Danube Delta to an underground cave, wildlife thrives.

*Opposite:* **Forests cover much of the land in Romania's mountains.**

## A Land of Trees and Farms

Forests cover more than one-fourth of Romania's land, particularly in the mountains. The altitude determines the types of trees. The lowest level has mainly deciduous trees, especially oak. Others are beech, elm, ash, sycamore, maple, hornbeam, and linden. Ferns and grasses grow in woodland clearings. From an altitude of about 2,600 to 4,600 feet (792 to 1,402 m), beech trees dominate. From there up to about 6,000 feet (1,829 m), conifers cover the land. Higher altitudes have mostly alpine and sub-alpine pastures. Vegetation is sparse—only mosslike plants and grasses grow there, along with a few hardy wildflowers.

A few places in Romania's mountain forests are about the only spots left untouched by humans. On the plateaus and in the plains, very little original vegetation remains. Agriculture, grazing, forestry, and human settlements have all made major changes to the landscape. Pastures cover 21 percent of the land while 41 percent is used for agricultural planting. About 10 percent consists of urban development and coastland.

## National Parks

The first of Romania's many beautiful national parks were established amid the splendor of the southern Carpathians in the 1930s. Among these is one of the largest, the Retezat (RE-tay-zat) National Park. It has more than eighty glacial lakes and covers more than 140,000 acres (56,700 hectares). Romania has nearly 600 nature reserves. A few are large, but most are smaller forested parks, animal preserves, and paleontological and geological sites. Every large urban area has a forested park nearby.

Once the hills of the Moldavian plateau were covered with forests, but the timber industry took many of the trees. As a result, with each strong wind or heavy rain, more of the hillsides wash down into the valley. This erosion has removed much of the fertile topsoil, so it is difficult to replant seedlings that will grow into healthy, strong trees with roots to hold the soil in place. Romanians are working to meet this challenge by planting a belt of trees at upper elevations, helping to prevent further erosion. Despite these problems, Moldavia is still the most heavily forested region in Romania.

## Animals Aplenty

Among the many animals making their homes in Romania are some rare species. The chamois is a hoofed mammal found on the alpine heights of the Carpathians. Its upright horns have backward-hooked tips. Other animals of the mountain forests are red deer, brown bear, wolf, lynx, fox, wild pig, black goat, Carpathian stag, and marten. There are many songbirds in the mountains, too, along with woodcock, grouse, nightingale, and golden eagles. Polecats, squirrels, and foxes roam the valleys, and a few buffalo live by the rivers.

**Chamois live in the Carpathian Mountains.**

**A pine marten**

Bustards live in the plains.

The plains, however, are home to few animals—only a small number of foxes, rabbits, and small rodents. Birds are common, though, particularly pheasants, partridges, and crows. Bustards live here, too—these large birds can run along the ground faster than a horse!

## The Danube Delta

The Danube Delta is a large area in the Dobrogea region of Romania where the Danube River breaks into three large branches before flowing into the Black Sea. Along its route, the river picks up soil and debris that has been deposited here over the past 6,500 years, creating fertile patches of land between the three branches. This region covers about 1,750 square miles (4,532 sq km) and has a great diversity of plants and animals.

## Movile Cave

A unique habitat—the world's only ecosystem that does not rely on sunlight—was discovered in 1986 in southeastern Romania near the Black Sea. In Movile Cave, 80 feet (24 m) below ground and sealed off from the rest of the world for 5.5 million years, scientists found an ecosystem containing forty-eight species of animals such as leeches, millipedes, scorpions, and spiders. It is the only known ecosystem where plants and animals do not rely on photosynthesis (the natural process by which plants turn sunlight into energy). Photosynthesis makes plants the base of the food chain that supports an ecosystem.

The base of the food chain in Movile Cave, however, is the thick layer of bacteria that floats above 5 feet (1.5 m) of water at the bottom of the cave. All the animals in the cave either eat the bacteria or eat animals that eat the bacteria. The bacteria live on energy-rich molecules of hydrogen sulfide found in the rocks of the cave walls. The life forms in the cave get oxygen that flows in from the outside through tiny cracks in the rock, but that is their only connection to the outside world.

The cave was detected when engineers were drilling a new construction site. Researchers from the Speleological Institute in Bucharest made the amazing discovery.

Scientists believe similar ecosystems probably exist elsewhere on Earth—they just haven't been discovered yet. Even more exciting—scientists think that Movile Cave can serve as a model of possible life on Mars. They believe that if life does exist there, it has probably been sealed below ground for about 3.5 million years, dating back to an era when Mars was warmer and wetter.

Inland, much of the delta is very rich agricultural land. Romanian farmers use this soil to grow many crops—a variety of grains, many vegetables, including tomatoes, and fruits, such as grapes. Large fields of bright sunflowers also grow here.

Most of the Danube Delta is made up of swamp and marshes where the land is still shifting with the currents of the rivers. However, enough plants send down roots to make it

A reed bank on the Danube Delta

Polecats live along the banks of the Danube Delta.

somewhat stable. Floating reed islands—called *plaur*—help hold the soil in place. This marshy land is a perfect environment for bulrushes, cattails, and sedges. Water lilies and water hemlock also grow here in abundance.

With such a rich and varied landscape, it's no wonder that the Danube Delta is a haven for animals—a large variety of mammals, 300 species of birds, 2,000 species of insects, and 60 species of fish. Perhaps the most valuable fish is the sturgeon, which is plentiful along the Danube and in the delta. Its eggs—or roe—make the best caviar.

Otters live here along the riverbanks, along with wolves, hares, minks, ermine, muskrats, foxes, polecats, and wild boars. Some of the mammals have adapted to this wet environment, where flooding is frequent. The reed fox, for example, lives on the islets of floating reeds, from which it gets its name. Reed wolves live on the islets, too, preying on the smaller, weak, or injured animals in the delta. Tortoises and lizards are also found here.

Pelicans breed here in large numbers, and wild swans flock to the delta. Their food is plentiful in the pools and channels found in the swampy region. Frequently, they are joined by thousands of migratory birds—flocks of more than 200 species from northern Europe, Asia, and Africa stop in the delta for food and rest before heading onward. Pygmy cormorants are found here, too, along with great white herons, spoonbills, and mute swans. Glossy ibises, golden eagles, avocets, shelduck, reed buntings, whooper swans, plovers, arctic grebes, cranes, half snipes, egrets, Saker falcons, and mandarin ducks make their homes here at least part of the year. Even the rare white-tailed eagle can sometimes be seen in the delta.

## Problems on the Delta

In recent decades, the environmental health of the Danube Delta has faced serious challenges. Nicolae Ceaușescu, Romania's leader from 1965 to 1989, wanted to use all of Romania's resources to help the economy. The delta was a treasure trove for fishing, forestry, and agricultural projects.

Fishing was increased greatly, dangerously depleting some of the species. Thousands of trees were cut down and much of the Danube Delta's marshland was drained for farmland. Pesticides and fertilizers used by farmers threatened to pollute the waters. Plants and animals were dying.

For example, many pelicans disappeared though they once flourished in the delta. Pollution killed some and forced others to find new habitats. The pelicans had once feasted on weaker fish swimming in the delta's waters, but now the weak fish were left to pass on disease, and many fish species were dying out. The Danube Delta was in serious trouble.

When Ceaușescu's rule came to an end, help came to the delta. Environmental organizations from around the world joined together to plant trees, clean up the water, and return the farmland to its natural state. In 1990, the new Romanian government established the Danube Delta Biosphere Reserve. This reserve protects more than 193 square miles (500 sq km) from further industrialization.

Progress is being made, but money to fund environmental programs is hard to come by in Romania's shaky economy. And much more needs to be done before the Danube Delta returns to health.

# Oppression
# with
# Optimism

**H**UMANS HAVE LEFT THEIR MARK ON ROMANIA'S natural environment. People have occupied the land for more than 3,000 years—as settlers and conquerors, farmers and villagers, peasants and industrialists. This has affected society as well. Romania still reflects the imprints of those who came before.

*Opposite:* **The Palace at Bucharest in the Ottoman period**

**A Stone Age terracotta statue found in Romania**

### From Caves to Conquerors

Bones, tools, and weapons have been found deep in caves in the Carpathian Mountains. Left behind by hunters and gatherers during the Stone Age some 6,000 years ago, these are the only clues we have about the people who used them. The earliest recorded settlers on land that is now part of Romania were people called Dacians. They arrived during the European Iron Age, about 800 to 300 B.C.

The Dacians came from regions that are now India and Europe. They mainly occupied Transylvania, but in the first century B.C., they expanded their borders to the Danube River and the Black Sea.

Their control of this great sweep of land posed a threat to the Roman Empire, which was then taking over much of the region. In A.D. 106, after years of battle, the Romans conquered the

Dacians and in A.D. 107, the region became the Roman province of Dacia.

**Dacians retreating before the Romans**

Many Romans settled alongside native Dacians to enjoy the land's prosperity. Gold and grain alike were plentiful and supplied the Roman Empire. Dacians married Romans, and Roman culture began to flourish in the province. This influence was the beginning of what is sometimes called the "Romanization" of the region. People identified with the Romans, leading to their eventual unity as Romanians centuries later.

Romans controlled the region for more than 150 years. But in A.D. 271, they abandoned the land under pressure from fierce tribes invading from

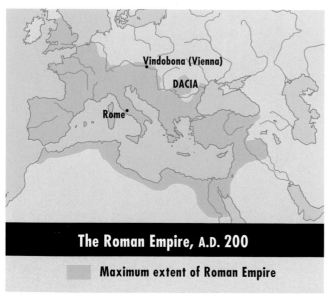

**The Roman Empire, A.D. 200**

Maximum extent of Roman Empire

the east. For the next 1,000 years, the people of the region withstood the arrival of many conquering tribes. There are no written records detailing what happened in the land we now know as Romania. But we know that Visigoths, Huns, Germanic-Gepidae, Avars, Slavs, Bulgars, Hungarians, Pechenegs, and Cumans all controlled parts of the region at one time. They either moved on or blended into the population, only to be conquered by another tribe. The Slavs, particularly, stayed on and married residents of the region.

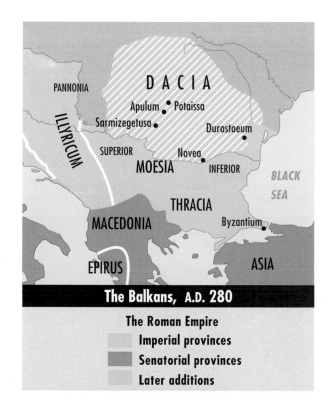

Each of these conquering tribes took over only a particular territory—never the whole of what is now Romania—so each area took on an identity of its own. This was the beginning of the six regions of Romania. The three largest ones today—Walachia, Moldavia, and Transylvania—were also the largest and strongest in 1250 to 1350, when they were beginning to emerge as independent regions.

During this period, Transylvania was controlled by Hungarians, also known as Magyars, and the many Romanian people who lived there were considered inferior. In Walachia, the people gradually united under a single ruler—a prince. A similar process took place in Moldavia. Both became principalities.

## Walachia and Moldavia

Walachia and Moldavia became parts of the Byzantine Empire, so much of their cultures and social patterns followed traditions from the East. Their independence didn't last long, though. During the fifteenth through nineteenth centuries, Turkish Ottoman armies advanced into Walachia and Moldavia, as well as much of southeastern Europe, and took hold.

A Moldavian prince, Michel Soutzo, in 1819

The principalities were able to retain some of their independence by paying the Ottoman leaders a steep annual tribute in money and resources. The Ottomans controlled their trade, selected their rulers, and guided international affairs for the people of the principalities, but let them keep control of their domestic affairs. Life was hard for the peasants under these conditions. They were barely able to provide for their own needs after paying off the Ottomans. But because of this sacrifice, they were able to keep most of their society intact and prevent a massive influx of Muslim culture by the Ottomans.

Over the centuries, the people of the principalities made several attempts to overthrow the Ottomans and regain control of their land. One of the most famous leaders was Mircea the Old, who lived from 1368 to 1418. He was a prince of Walachia who had some success in battles against the Turks. Because of this, Romanians still recall him as a brave and great leader.

But the Ottoman Turks were not to be defeated yet. Instead, they sent in wealthy Greeks, called Phanariots, to rule the principalities from the early 1700s to 1821. The Phanariots were ruthless, calling for more tribute than ever—not only money but products such as grain, honey, lumber, and sheep. It was an exceedingly difficult period for the peasants, but their revolts and rebellions seemed to gain strength with every difficulty forced upon them. Eventually, after many battles, the Ottomans gave in and removed the Phanariot rulers, replacing them with local princes.

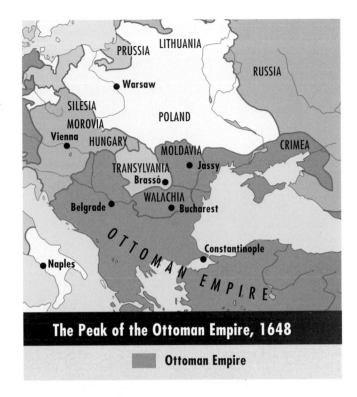

**The Peak of the Ottoman Empire, 1648**

Ottoman Empire

In 1829, Russian troops took over the principalities of Walachia and Moldavia. Though their occupation lasted only five years and the Turks retained official control, the Russians set in place the first representative government in Romania—an assembly chosen to lead each principality. The Turkish Ottomans retained official control until 1878 but actually had little influence.

Throughout the history of Moldavia and Walachia, many people wanted to unite the two principalities as one nation. Supporters of unification, sometimes called nationalists, spent years promoting their cause within the principalities and throughout the rest of Europe. By the late 1850s, as Turkish control of the two principalities was waning, there was a rise in nationalism—citizens felt free to express their desire to unite. Most recognized their common ancestry dating back to Roman rule, and they considered themselves Romanian. Leaders took more than two years to work out the details, but finally, in 1859, a ruler was selected, Prince Alexandru Ioan Cuza. Walachia and Moldavia, now known as the United Principalities, became the nation of Romania in 1861.

**Prince Alexandru Ioan Cuza**

At this time, revolutionary changes were taking place throughout Europe. People were demanding a more fair system of government in which the rights of all people would be respected. In response, Prince Alexandru made changes to benefit the poor. He took land from the wealthy nobles and religious monasteries and granted greater freedom to peasants who had been forced to work those lands. He opened free schools for all children. Prince Alexandru was popular with the peasants, but in 1866, the wealthy ruling class forced him to leave the throne.

He was replaced by a more moderate prince, Carol of Hohenzollern-Sigmaringen, of Germany. (Some histories refer to him as Charles, rather than Carol.) Under his rule, all citizens could vote. However, not all residents were considered citizens, especially the large Jewish minority and other non-Christians. They were not allowed to own land in rural areas either. As a result, many Jews had no choice but to congregate in cities, and many made their livings by operating small businesses.

In May 1877, Romania declared its independence from the Turks, and the Turks granted it the following year. At this time, Jews were granted citizenship, too. Three years later, when Romania became a kingdom, Prince Carol became King Carol I.

**King Carol I in 1877**

During his reign, King Carol did much to improve Romania's economy and brought the country's industries up to date. Yet he had little regard for Romania's poor and made sure that money stayed in the hands of the wealthy. The differences in lifestyle between wealthy city inhabitants and rural peasants grew. Cities were becoming modernized—privileged Bucharest citizens, for example, enjoyed running water and sewers and electric streetcars by the 1890s. But the peasants who paid the taxes that helped supply these benefits to the cities still struggled in poverty.

**The 1907 peasant uprising**

The peasants' anger simmered for years. In 1888, and again in 1907, they revolted. Throughout the country, property of the wealthy was destroyed—homes were burned, fields were ravaged. But each time, the final blow was dealt by the Romanian Army, which killed more than 10,000 peasants to halt the rebellions.

The Romanian Army was also involved in the second Balkan War in 1913 and forced Bulgaria to turn over the Dobrogea region to Romania. This was a major acquisition because Dobrogea provides access to the Black Sea. King Carol died in 1914, the year World War I began.

### Queen Marie

One of Romania's most beloved rulers was Queen Marie. Born in Great Britain in 1875, she was a granddaughter of Britain's Queen Victoria and the oldest daughter of the Duke and Duchess of Edinburgh. When she was seventeen, she married Ferdinand, who was in line to become king of Romania. Though her Romanian life was far different from her life in Britain, she grew to deeply love her adopted country.

During the second Balkan War in 1913, while still a princess, Marie ran a cholera hospital for Romanian soldiers. When King Carol I died in 1914, Ferdinand I and Marie became king and queen. Even as queen, she continued to work in Bucharest hospitals, making daily rounds of the wards housing wounded soldiers. She kept crosses in her apron pocket to give to those

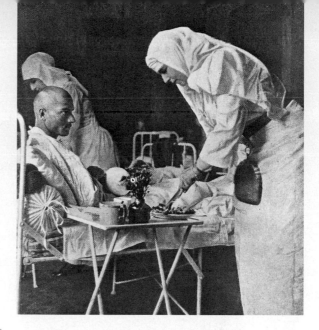

who were near death. Marie and Ferdinand had five children. While raising them and helping to run the country, she also published fifteen books, ranging from fairy tales and romances to travelogues and an autobiography. Queen Marie died in 1938.

## Transylvania

Transylvania was also undergoing political changes during the long period when Moldavia and Walachia were controlled by the Turkish Ottomans until they won independence in 1878. Transylvania was held by Hungary until the Ottoman Turks defeated Hungary in 1526. But unlike Moldavia and Walachia, Transylvania was left much on its own by the Ottomans. Though the region paid tribute to Turkey, it was a principality and selected its own rulers. In 1688, Transylvanian leaders seeking more religious tolerance and economic reforms defied the Turks and agreed to come under control of Austria's Habsburg Empire. Because of its many natural resources, Transylvania was generally better off than

Moldavia and Walachia. However, the wealth often stayed in the hands of the landowners. Peasants, both Hungarians and Romanians, continued to live in dreadful poverty.

The peasants' anger finally led to revolt, as it had in the other two regions. In 1784, 1819, and throughout most of the 1840s, peasants rebelled against the wealthy landowners. Though the peasants caused much damage to property, the wealthy prevailed. In 1848, the Hungarian rulers decided to make Transylvania a part of Hungary, and Austrian rule came to an end. Thousands of Romanian peasants then demanded their independence and announced their desire to form a union with Moldavia and Walachia.

Their demands were ignored, and Hungary retained control. By the late 1800s, Hungarian rulers were determined to put an end to further rebellions through severe restrictions on all the ethnic minorities in Transylvania. But World War I interfered with those plans.

## World War I

World War I began in 1914. After King Carol died, he was succeeded by his nephew, King Ferdinand, who kept Romania out of the fray for two years. In 1916, Romania joined the war on the side of the Allies led by Great Britain and France. Almost immediately, enemy troops from the Central Powers—Bulgaria, Austria, and Hungary—descended upon Romania and took control. Romania was forced to sign the May 1918 Treaty of Bucharest. This treaty forced Romania to return Dobrogea to Bulgaria, and parts of the Carpathian

Mountain region bordering Transylvania were granted to Austria and Hungary.

The Romanian Army quickly geared up again and returned to battle in time to rejoin the Allied forces in the final victory. In the peace plans agreed to in November 1918, Romanians received Transylvania from Hungary. Two years later, as part of the settlement, Romania also acquired the Bukovina and Banat regions and land to the north of Transylvania and east of Moldavia. These areas all contained large populations of Romanian people. In all, the additional land more than doubled the size and population of Romania.

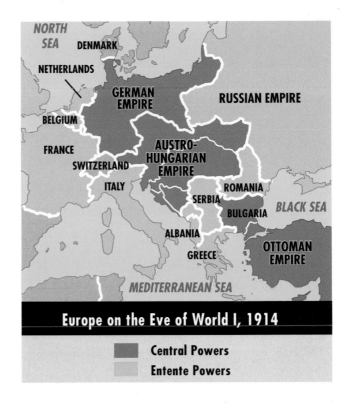

**Europe on the Eve of World I, 1914**

Central Powers
Entente Powers

Romanian dead line a railway embankment in World War I.

Following World War I, Romanian leaders made an attempt to settle the revolts by the peasants. They also were faced with problems from the Hungarian people living in Transylvania, which was now part of Romania. Minorities, especially Hungarian Jews, were discriminated against. Most Hungarians refused to cooperate with Romanian laws and government. Instead, they demanded political freedom.

King Ferdinand remained on the throne, but liberal political parties took charge and began working to assist peasants. Large tracts of land owned by wealthy non-Romanians were taken by the government, broken up into smaller units, and sold to the Romanian peasants that had worked on them. In all, 15 million acres (6 million ha) went from large to small landowners. Additional programs to aid the poor were also put into place. People were allowed to select their own local leaders.

But in 1929, economic hard times hit the country and the world. The Great Depression that caused so much hardship in the United States created similar problems in many other countries. Millions of workers lost their jobs, people lost their savings, and the Romanian government had little funding to help. Part of the economic problem in Romania was caused by the land reforms that the people had welcomed only a few years earlier. When peasants took over agricultural land, they did not have the technology or the machinery that the previous owners—wealthy farmers—had. They were unable to grow as much grain as had been produced in earlier years. They also faced competition trading grain around the world because more developed countries, especially the United States, could produce so much more. So the country's main export—grain—no longer brought much money into the country.

These economic troubles made the Romanian people look for a new direction in leadership. Liberal policies, it seemed, had caused only extreme poverty. And the country's royalty at the time offered little direction. King Ferdinand had died in 1927 and his son, Carol, who was next in line for the throne, left the country with his mistress. Carol's six-year-old son Michael was placed in charge, but he was too young to offer any leadership. A select group of people, called a regency, made decisions for him.

Members of the fascist Iron Guard on parade in Bucharest

During this time, Romania had an unsettled political climate—perfect for someone offering strong direction to step in. Corneliu Codreanu, the founder of a fascist organization called the Iron Guard, assumed leadership. He set up a strong government that demanded total obedience but also portrayed itself as a defender of the country of Romania. His followers in the Iron Guard were encouraged to be violent, even to kill their opponents. Jews were harassed and so were members of royalty and political liberals. This harassment appealed to many Romanian peasants who were tired of being trampled by foreign invaders and weakened by ineffective leaders.

King Carol II with his wife
and Crown Prince Michael

Carol, who had turned down his chance to be king, changed his mind and returned to Romania in 1930 as King Carol II. He first tried to cooperate with the Iron Guard, but because he wasn't willing to share power, he declared the party to be illegal. Most of the Iron Guard's 18,000 members were sent to prison in 1933. Codreanu and several of his close associates were killed in 1938, allegedly during an escape attempt. That same year, King Carol II declared a royal dictatorship, placing the monarchy squarely in charge of the country, and making all political parties illegal.

## World War II

In 1939, World War II began in Europe, where Nazi Germany and, later, other Axis countries fought the Allies—several nations led by Great Britain and France. Romania remained neutral at first, but as the fighting grew, King Carol II sensed a need to join with stronger countries to protect Romania's borders. France and Britain had agreed to help protect Romania, but in 1940, Germany seemed to be winning the war, and France fell to the Nazis. Romania was again forced to give up some of its land. Much of northeastern Romania went to the Soviet Union, one of the Allies. Northern Transylvania, where more than a million Romanians lived, was turned over

Soldiers in the Tatra Mountains during World War II

Premier Ion Antonescu (center) and King Michael (right) on the front in World War II

to Hungary, and parts of southeastern Romania went to Bulgaria, both Axis countries.

This loss of land outraged Romanians. Following their angry demands, King Carol II gave up his throne to his son Michael, but true leadership of the country went to Ion Antonescu, a respected general. He held the title *premier*, but ruled as a military dictator. Under his leadership, Romania entered the war on the side of Germany, providing food, oil, and other supplies to the Nazis. Romania joined the German invasion of the Soviet Union in an effort to regain the land it had lost to that country. Antonescu believed Germany would help Romania regain the territory it had lost in Transylvania also. Nearly half a million Romanian soldiers lost their lives in the war on the side of Germany, but only a small portion of Bukovina was returned to Romania.

King Michael, angry over the losses, bitter that Germany was not returning the territory to Romania, and fearing that Germany was beginning to lose the war, secretly started negotiations with the Allies. He switched sides, hoping for a better outcome for Romania when the war ended. In August 1944, the Soviet Red Army entered Romania and took control of Bucharest. Antonescu was arrested, and the new government joined with the Allies in the fight against Germany. In return, northern Transylvania rejoined Romania, but the Soviet Union kept the land it took from northeastern Romania, and Bulgaria retained its holdings in Dobrogea. Antonescu, meanwhile, faced a military trial in 1946 and was sentenced to death. He was executed on June 1, 1946.

## Communist Romania

When the Soviet Red Army entered Bucharest, it marked the beginnings of the communist hold on Romania. Not many Romanians supported communism at the time, and although communist candidates ran in the 1944 elections, they didn't win. The Soviets rigged the 1946 elections, making sure that communists became the majority party in Romania. Petru Groza led the government. Many of their opponents fled, others were thrown into prison, and some were killed. In 1947, King Michael was forced off the throne.

Romania was declared a People's Republic. Actually, it was a Soviet satellite, controlled by the Soviet Union. After this, there was little Western influence on Romanian life. Instead, the Soviet way became the model for such things as education, business, politics, health care, economics, and foreign policy. Agriculture, for example, became the key to the nation's economy and was run by the government. Romania's industry, which had been gaining strength, was also taken over by the state. Citizens suffered shortages of supplies, as most resources were sent directly to the Soviet Union. Even the arts were affected—painters, writers, and other artists had to abandon their ideas, and instead, create art that supported the Soviet ideals of communism.

Throughout history, Romanians often lived under the control of foreigners. But they were never content with this arrangement, and Soviet domination was no different.

Gheorghe Gheorghiu-Dej (holding flowers) visiting a hydroelectric plant under construction

Opposition to Soviet rule grew throughout the late 1940s and 1950s. Gheorghe Gheorghiu-Dej was head of the Romanian Communist Party during this period. He began the resistance to Soviet control, pushing for national communism instead. He and the Romanian communists insisted that all communist countries should be free to pursue their own economic policies,

**Eastern Europe, 1945–1990**

- Occupied by the Soviet Union
- Soviet Bloc countries 1945–1990
- — Iron Curtain

rather than follow Soviet rule. Soon, Romania began expanding its industry and trading with non-communist nations in the West. After Gheorghiu-Dej's death in 1965, Nicolae Ceauşescu continued expanding Romania's ties to the Western world.

Ceauşescu promised that more goods would become available to consumers. Though this never happened, areas such as education and health care improved. Artists were again free to pursue their own ideas. More and more, Western ideas and culture were expressed in Romania. The Soviet Union didn't see Romania as a significant threat to the overall strength of their communist agenda, so these rebellions were largely ignored.

But these were not the beginnings of good times for Romania. This time, trouble did not come in the form of a foreign invader, but from the abuse of power by one of their own—Ceauşescu.

### Ceauşescu's Cruel Reign

In the early years of his rule, Ceauşescu was accepted by most Romanians. He exercised little control over intellectuals and economic leaders. In 1968, he gained the admiration of

Romanians and others around the world when he spoke out against the Soviet invasion of Czechoslovakia. After President Richard Nixon of the United States visited Romania the next year, Ceaușescu earned even more stature as a leader.

But over time, he became greedy and corrupt. He loved power. Ceaușescu imposed harsh regulations on the Romanian people, controlling nearly every aspect of their lives. He feared losing his authority and grew paranoid. Anyone speaking out against him faced severe punishment. His wife, Elena, became more powerful, too. A vengeful woman who grew up poor, she now demanded the finest of everything, even while the Romanian people had no heat in their homes and no food for their families. People grew to hate them both as they continued to live lavishly in elegant palaces throughout the country.

In the early 1980s, Ceaușescu decided that Romania needed to pay off

**Elena and Nicolae Ceaușescu**

its debts to other countries within ten years. To achieve this goal, he increased exports while denying Romanians the products they needed to live even minimally decent lives. Most of the power produced was sold to other countries while Romanians were limited to one forty-watt bulb per room and could heat their homes only up to about 50° F (10° C)—when there was any heat at all. Food was scarce, as were clothes, appliances, and most other consumer goods. The national debt was being paid off, but at a great cost to Romanian citizens. Ceaușescu justified it all by suggesting that his fellow citizens were too fat anyway and were better off eating less.

During this time, Ceaușescu began to build an enormous "People's Palace" in which he intended to house all of the government. Although it was supposed to be the world's largest building, it is slightly smaller than the Pentagon in Washington, D.C. To make room for the palace and the grand "Victory of Socialism Boulevard" leading up to it, Ceaușescu had an entire district in Bucharest demolished. Here, 40,000 people had lived in charming homes, surrounded by historic churches and lovely

People lined up to buy the few loaves of bread for sale in a shop in 1981.

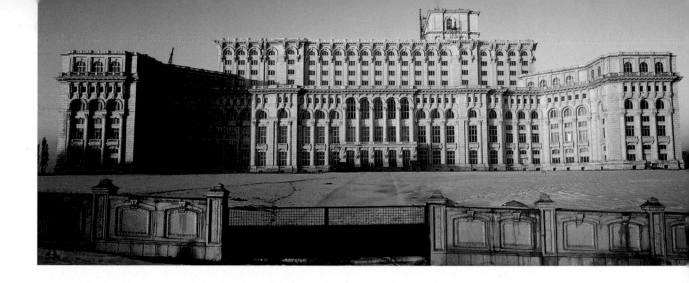

orchards. In their place, sterile government buildings and a 6,000-room palace, considered to be one of the ugliest buildings in the world, were built.

## The End of the Line

Perhaps Ceauşescu should have known this couldn't last forever; that the people would finally revolt, even under his harsh control. But he seemed oblivious to the signs.

On December 15, 1989, a protest began to grow in the town of Timişoara. A popular Reformed Church minister, the Reverend Lászlo Tökes, refused an order to leave his church. The order came from the Romanian Secret Police, the Securitate, which had long harassed him for his insistence on human rights. His defiance of the Securitate stirred the confidence of his followers who took to the streets in his support. The crowds grew the next day, as large groups of students, workers, and other citizens joined in—thousands of voices denouncing Ceauşescu and communism.

Ceauşescu ordered his troops to shut it down and personally ordered the killings that brought the protest to an end.

No one knows exactly how many people were killed—some said as many as 60,000, while other reports listed fewer than 700. Historical documents that could shed more light were destroyed. But in any case, Romanian rage over the massacre grew.

Still, Ceauşescu went on with his normal schedule. On December 20, 1989, he addressed the nation and blamed the uprising on "hooligans," praising the police and military who brought the disturbance to an end. He went on to warn that all demonstrators would be shot—a pronouncement that was the final straw to many citizens. Their outrage at his corruption finally became greater than their fear.

The next day, Ceauşescu staged a huge demonstration of his popular support. He had done this several times in the past—forcing thousands of citizens to attend rallies in his honor, where they were made to shout slogans of his greatness. These were shown on television as "proof" of the love of his fellow citizens.

But this time, those citizens were fed up, and their anger was caught on videotape. The words of praise they had been instructed to shout quickly turned to boos and screams of hatred. Ceauşescu, addressing the crowd, displayed confusion, while Elena, at his side, instructed the crowd to calm down. Then the state-run television cameras shut down and screens went blank for several minutes. When transmission resumed, Ceauşescu was still addressing the crowd, making empty promises that he believed would placate them, but it was clear that sentiments had changed.

Anti-Ceaușescu demonstrations erupted around the country. Some units of the Romanian Army switched sides, joining the protesters, and took over the state-run television station. Ceaușescu and his wife made a desperate attempt to flee the country, but on December 22 they were captured. Leaders of a newly formed organization, called National Salvation Front, took charge of the revolution and held a speedy military trial in which the Ceaușescus were found guilty of crimes against their country. Both of them were executed on Christmas Day.

An army tank and protesters fighting pro-Ceaușescu troops in Bucharest

### Doina Cornea

One of the most important and fearless critics of Ceaușescu and his policies was Doina Cornea, a teacher from Cluj. She was outraged at the way farmers were forced into substandard housing in cities so that the government could take over their land, and she was infuriated with the poverty Ceaușescu forced upon her fellow Romanians. She frequently wrote letters expressing her views and smuggled them out of Romania to the free press in other European nations, so that people around the world would know what was happening in her land. After she was detected by Romanian police, Cornea was closely watched, and at

times severely beaten, but she refused to give up. Her letters helped to build support around the world for her cause—to get rid of Ceaușescu.

# Starting Over, Getting It Right

"**G**OD HAS TURNED HIS FACE TOWARD ROMANIA again." These were the first words spoken on Romanian radio on December 22, 1989, when it was free to broadcast openly following the fall of the Ceauşescu regime. Mircea Dinescu, a poet who had long fought against the Ceauşescus, gave voice to the hopes of all Romanians when he spoke those words. The Romanian people had a chance to start over, to create—at last—a government that was fair and honest.

*Opposite:* **The National Assembly building**

### A New Leader for New Times

Ion Iliescu became Romania's interim—temporary—president in 1989, following the deaths of the Ceauşescus. He was head of the National Salvation Front (NSF), the group that led the overthrow. They changed the country's name from the Socialist Republic of Romania to Romania.

**Ion Iliescu**

The NSF began a ten-point program to bring positive changes to Romania. The program called for a democratic form of government, which would not allow any one single political party to take complete control; free elections; and separation of powers among the various levels of government. It also called for the end of government control of businesses and agriculture and the promotion of entrepreneurship among the citizens; a new system of education; rights and freedoms for ethnic minorities; and a national foreign policy in the best interest of Romanian citizens.

The NSF quickly made other positive changes. The death penalty was ended. Romanians were allowed to travel outside the country more freely. Food that was to have been exported out of the country went to Romanian shops instead. Houses were heated again. People were allowed to practice their religion freely. In the few short months following the revolution, things began to look up for the country.

However, many problems remained. Ethnic differences emerged, particularly with the Hungarians. And although some immediate prosperity followed the end of the Ceauşescu reign, the long-term situation was bleak. It was impossible to turn the economy around quickly. In a few months, homes were again without heat, and people were again going hungry. On May 20, 1990, in the midst of all the changes, Romania also held its first free elections. Iliescu received 85 percent of the vote to become president. He and other government leaders went to work creating a new Constitution for Romania. It was adopted in late 1991.

**Voting in Romania's first free elections**

### The Constitution

Romania is a parliamentary republic, according to its Constitution. Its top government official is the president, who is elected by popular vote for up to two four-year terms.

He watches over the public authorities, represents Romania to the world, and commands the military and national defense. The president appoints a prime minister, who then selects and leads the eighteen cabinet members of the Council of Ministers. Their selection must be validated by a vote of the parliament. The cabinet members carry out the various functions of government, including both domestic and foreign policy.

Romania's parliament, called the National Assembly, consists of a Senate, with 143 members, and a 343-member Chamber of Deputies. All representatives to the National Assembly are elected to four-year terms. They come from each of the country's 41 administrative units under a system of

**The National Assembly in session**

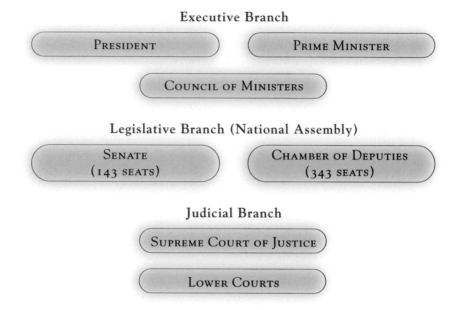

**NATIONAL GOVERNMENT OF ROMANIA**

Executive Branch

PRESIDENT

PRIME MINISTER

COUNCIL OF MINISTERS

Legislative Branch (National Assembly)

SENATE
(143 SEATS)

CHAMBER OF DEPUTIES
(343 SEATS)

Judicial Branch

SUPREME COURT OF JUSTICE

LOWER COURTS

proportional representation—units with more people have more representatives in Parliament.

Romania's 41 administrative units are actually 40 counties and 1 special district—the capital city of Bucharest. Each unit has its own local government, as do cities, towns, and communes—rural areas within the counties.

## The Judiciary

The legal system—the judiciary—is a separate branch of the government, just as it is in the United States. The Supreme Court of Justice is Romania's highest court. Its members, appointed by the president, hear appeals from the lower county courts. There are also local courts and military courts.

Each of the nation's 41 administrative units has its own county court and several local courts. Judges are independent and are sworn to obey the law, not any political leader.

The public interest is guarded by the Public Ministry, a group of lawyers that maintain order under the law and represent society's general interests, freedoms, and rights. These lawyers are similar to attorneys general in the United States.

## Armed Forces

Romania maintains a military force with an army, navy, and air force. Men over age eighteen are drafted, usually for sixteen months. As of 1997, there were about 227,000 men on active duty.

**Soldiers on parade**

In 1992, Ion Iliescu was reelected president, but the 1996 presidential election was won by Emil Constantinescu, a professor and leader of the Romanian Democratic Convention. Under Constantinescu's leadership, the government established

## Emil Constantinescu

It's not just the people of Romania that interest President Emil Constantinescu, but the ground beneath them as well. He was trained as a geologist. Rocks and minerals are an unusual occupation for a politician, but Constantinescu hopes to be an unusual leader for Romania—one who is guided by the needs of the nation and will lead the citizens to peace and prosperity.

Constantinescu was born in 1939. He received a law degree in 1960 and served for a brief time as a judge, but in 1961 he gave up the law. Romania's communist leaders placed too many restrictions on the judicial system, he believed, so he became a geologist instead. He taught at the University of Bucharest for more than twenty-five years and lectured around the world. Still, his interest in the law and politics remained keen.

When the Ceaușescu reign came to an end in late 1989, Constantinescu was instrumental in founding the Universitarian Society, a group of Romanian university professors and students who believed in democracy for their nation. He helped create the Steering Committee of the Civic Alliance, another organization that sought democracy in Romania and also worked for cooperation among the ethnic minorities in the country.

Constantinescu ran for president in 1992 but lost to Ion Iliescu. Still, he continued his political involvement within the Romanian Democratic Convention. When he ran again in 1996, stating his intent to get rid of government corruption, promote private industry, build the economy, and improve international relations, he won. He admits that it has not been easy to create change in Romanian life, but he remains committed.

"After the sacrifices and toil of successive generations," Constantinescu said in 1998, "after so many pains and sufferings engendered by dictatorships, after the sacrifice of the Revolution, now the citizens of Romania have the right to work and live peacefully, fearlessly, they have the right to commit themselves to a destiny rooted in their own option and answering their own aspirations."

the 1998–2000 program, a map for progress into the next century. It describes a government that works to better the economy at the regional and local levels; to increase understanding and cohesion among all citizens, including the ethnic minorities; and to improve the image of Romania around the world.

Romania is working to build its international reputation. It is a member of the United Nations and the Council of Europe and is expected to become a full member of the North Atlantic Treaty Organization (NATO). Currently, Romania is a member of the Partnership for Peace program, a necessary step toward NATO membership. Romania supported NATO during its conflict with Yugoslavia by offering its airspace. President Constantinescu traveled to Washington, D.C. in April 1999, for the international summit marking NATO's fiftieth anniversary.

While the road map for peace, freedom, and economic security has been laid out for Romania, not all of

## The National Anthem

"Awaken Thee, Romanian," was written for the 1848 Revolution by Romanian poet Andrei Mureşan. The anthem encourages Romanians to rise up and fight off invaders for the glory of their ancestors and their homeland. Its words are still fitting for the struggles facing Romanians today. The song has been sung at many crucial moments in the nation's history. It gave Romanians courage during the Independence War in 1877–1878 and during both world wars when their homeland was threatened. During the 1989 revolution to end Ceauşescu's rule, there are reports that masses of citizens began to sing the anthem spontaneously.

"Awaken Thee, Romanian"
Awaken thee, Romanian, shake off the deadly slumber.
The scourge of inauspicious barbarian tyrannies
And now or never to a bright horizon clamber
That shall to shame put all your nocuous enemies.
It's now or never to the world we readily proclaim
In our veins throbs an ancestry of Roman
And in our hearts for ever we glorify a name
Resounding of battle, the name of gallant Trajan.
Do look imperial shadows, Michael, Stephen, Corvinus
At the Romanian nation, your mighty progeny
With arms like steel and hearts of fire impetuous
It's either free or dead, that's what they all decree.
Priests, rise the cross, this Christian army's liberating
The word is freedom, no less sacred is the end
We'd rather die in battle, in elevated glory
Than live again enslaved on our ancestral land.

its people are satisfied with the pace of change. In the spring of 1999, thousands of trade-union members turned out for rallies in several Romanian cities to protest government policies they felt were holding them back economically. At least 10,000 people gathered in Bucharest, calling for new labor laws, better wages, lower utility prices, and a grace period for companies unable to pay their debts.

But most people hope that political and economic stability will come along eventually. At the close of 1998, President Emil Constantinescu spoke to the Romanian people about the difficulty of the nation's reforms and his confidence about the future. "If next year these processes go on at the same pace that they have been evolving in the last months, there is a chance that the Romanians might start to see the fruit of the sacrifices they have been making ever since 1989."

## The National Flag

Blue, yellow, and red are the colors that have symbolized Romania on its flag for hundreds of years. Since the

Revolution of 1848, these colors are vertical stripes on the flag, each an equal third. At various times in history, the stripes were horizontal, and they were not always of equal size, but the colors have never changed.

During communist rule, a communist emblem was emblazoned on the center yellow stripe of the flag. But in the 1989 Revolution, as communist rule was coming to an end, protestors cut the emblem out of the flag. Romanian flags with holes cut out were a powerful symbol of national unity in this turbulent time. One of the first official acts following the revolution was to permanently remove the emblem from the flag.

## Bucharest: Did You Know This?

Acording to legend, Romania's capital took its name from its supposed founder, a shepherd named Bucar. Bucharest lies on plains between the Danube River and the Carpathian Mountains. It was the capital of Walachia in the seventeenth to nineteenth centuries and became capital of Romania in 1862. Today, it has a population of 2.4 million. One of Bucharest's nicknames is "the Garden City," thanks to the lovely parks and lush vegetation found throughout its borders.

The city still retains much of its original architectural beauty, but it no longer has the elegance it did prior to World War II, when it was called the "Paris of the East." Bombings during the war, earthquakes, and bulldozers have robbed the city of some of its historical loveliness. During the final years of his reign, Nicolae Ceaușescu ordered bulldozers to raze more than 7,000 homes and 15 churches in the historic district of the city, to make room for a building second in size only to the Pentagon in Washington, D.C. Its 6,000 rooms were intended to house Ceaușescu's office and other government headquarters, but Ceaușescu was executed shortly before it was completed. Ion Iliescu finished building it and turned it into an international conference center.

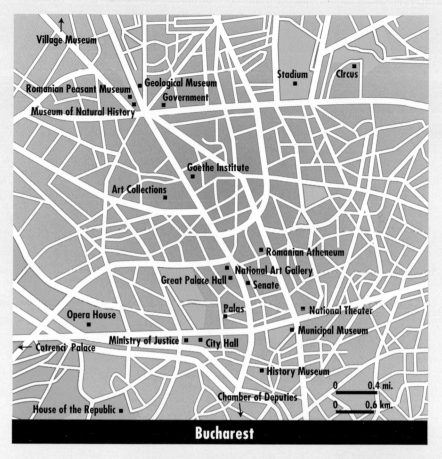

# An Evolving Economy

$F$OLLOWING THE REVOLUTION OF 1989, ROMANIANS WERE thrilled when the restrictions on their economy were lifted. The government was no longer in charge of all business and industry—individuals could run their own businesses. Food was again available for sale, along with other goods that had been stockpiled or exported to other countries by the Ceauşescu regime. People had heat in their homes, too.

But the challenges of shifting the economy away from communism have proved great. Within a few months, produce and fuel were again in short supply. And the value of Romanian currency, the *leu*, dropped drastically, while prices of essential goods climbed rapidly over the course of several years. This inflation made products so expensive that most peo-

The *leu* is Romania's basic unit of currency.

ple could not afford to purchase the basic necessities of life. Romanians were even worse off than they had been under Ceauşescu.

## Moving to Privatization

In 1990, the government established the National Agency for Privatization, and it passed laws in 1991 requiring state-owned

**Farm fields at harvest time**

businesses to be sold to private investors. So far, most privatization—or sale to private individuals—has been in the areas of agriculture and small business. Most of Romania's farmland is now individually owned—in fact, most of it has been returned to the farmers from whom it was taken in the first place. About 75 percent of the country's retail business is run by individuals as well. But only about 20 percent of the nation's industry is in the hands of the private sector.

One reason the large enterprises are shifting ownership so slowly is that the people most likely to buy them are top-level government officials. They are usually the only ones with the right connections and enough money. But these officials have little incentive to move quickly, fearing they might cause resentment on the part of their colleagues and therefore lose government privileges. Many government officials are also reluctant to turn over industry to private individuals because they enjoy the power they have. If industry is in the hands of individuals, the government loses much of its control on the economy.

Some large industries receive heavy government subsidies, which would be dropped if the industry were privatized. This could cause huge price increases and a loss of jobs within the industry.

One example of this is coal mining. For many years, the mining industry had not turned a large profit, but because of financial support from the government, miners were among the highest paid Romanian workers. What would happen without government subsidies? Would miners' wages go down? Would they lose their jobs? No one is willing to anger the large and powerful miners'

**Miners are well paid in Romania.**

## Romanian Money

The main unit of money in Romania is the *leu*, which means "lion" in Romanian. The plural is *lei*. Coins come in denominations of up to 100 lei, and bills are in denominations of up to 10,000 lei. The leu is actually divided up into 100 bani, but the bani is worth so little that these coins are basically worthless and never used.

Romanian coins typically have the head of a past leader imprinted on the front—in particular, Kings Carol I, Carol II, Michael, and Ştefan cel Mare. Another coin honors Prince Cuza, who led the united Moldavia and Walachia. On the backs of coins, the amount is noted, and the crest of Romania is also printed. The 2,000-lei bill features the August 1999 solar eclipse.

**Resources**

| | | | | | |
|---|---|---|---|---|---|
| | Cereals | **Ag** | Silver | **Cu** | Copper |
| | Farming | **Al** | Bauxite | **I** | Iron |
| | Pasture | **Au** | Gold | **O** | Oil |
| | Forests | **C** | Coal | **S** | Salt |

union. In 1997, the government made an offer to miners that many seized on—it would pay money to miners willing to retire voluntarily. About 15,000 stepped forward, showing that many probably believe that their jobs are in jeopardy.

## An Industrious Future

There is reason for some optimism that eventually, the country's economic problems will be solved. The nation has many natural resources, hardworking people, and an industrial base.

Romania's natural resources aid its economy and its ability to provide for itself. In fact, the largest energy resources in southeast Europe are found in Romania—particularly oil and gas, retrieved from offshore wells; and coal, uranium, and hydropower. Natural gases, too, are found Transylvania. More than 70 percent of Romania's power needs are met by domestic resources. Romania even has a nuclear power plant, built with the help of Canada and Italy, which began operation in 1996.

Romania has had a metals industry for centuries. When Romans occupied the land, gold and silver were mined in the southern portion of the region. Other valuable minerals include salt, copper, manganese, iron, molybdenum, uranium, and zirconium. This industry, however, brings environmental problems to Romania. Emissions from smelting plants pour out harmful fumes containing toxins such as lead, zinc, arsenic, and cadmium. Workers inside the plants wear neither protective clothing nor breathing apparati. Thousands of people living near such plants visit sanitariums each year to recover from poisoning caused by breathing these poisonous fumes.

Forestry is a profitable industry in Romania. Forests cover more than one-quarter of the land. Oak and beech are hardwoods used in the furniture industry, and other woods are used in construction, boat-building, and the manufacture of musical instruments.

Workers in the forestry industry

The fishing industry in Romania, though relatively small, is strong, thanks to the country's access to the Danube Delta and the Black Sea. There is a heavy demand for fresh fish within the country, so most of each catch is used domestically within a few days. But some fish is canned for later use and for export.

**Fishing for sturgeon on the Danube Delta**

**Working in a machine tool factory**

One of the most important sectors in Romanian industry is the production of foodstuffs. Much of it is for Romanian consumption, and most of the rest is exported to other countries in central and eastern Europe. Beer and wines from Romania are well-received throughout the world.

Another major component of Romanian industry is mechanical engineering and the manufacture of simple machines and component parts for large machines. Also important are the textile and clothing industry and the manufacture of shoes and other leather goods. Romania also manufactures fertilizer, cement, steel, pig iron, and aluminum.

## Science Needs to Catch Up

One factor standing in the way of a strong Romanian economy is its slow scientific advances. Romania has been left behind, thanks in large part to Nicolae Ceauşescu's wife, Elena. Though she'd had little formal training, she considered herself a great scientist and declared herself the nation's "First Chemist." She took control of the Romanian Academy, where most scientific research was centered, and drastically cut its funding. She shifted its efforts away from research to promoting her husband's government. Most Romanian scientists at the time swallowed their disgust and spoke her praises. They were afraid to challenge her for fear of losing their jobs, their freedom, or their lives.

When the Ceauşescu regime came to an end, the Romanian scientific community had fallen far behind the rest of the world in terms of funding, research, equipment, and training. It is struggling to catch up, particularly since the 1996 election of President Constantinescu, a scientist himself. But the government has many problems to contend with and can devote little time and resources into building up the scientific community.

Most scientists doing research in Romania right now must take a second job just to pay the bills. Funding from the international community seems to offer the best hope for the future. In the meantime, Romanian scientists are working to do whatever research they can and to encourage talented young scientists that may someday be able to compete on the world stage.

**Romania in Space**

Romania is pressing forward in outer space. The Romanian Space Agency (ROSA) is headed by the country's first cosmonaut, Dorin Prunariu, who flew on *Soyuz*, a Soviet space mission, in 1981. ROSA is actually a coalition of some forty scientific organizations within Romania carrying out work on the peaceful uses of space technology. Most current projects are directed toward the use of small satellite missions for communications and observations of Earth.

## Popular Foreign Investments

Do you enjoy drinking a Coca-Cola now and then? If you do, you have that in common with people from Romania. You have something else in common if you brush your teeth with Colgate toothpaste. These two foreign products have become commonplace in Romania.

As soon as restrictions on Romania's business community were lifted, Coca-Cola was one of the first large, international businesses to establish itself there. Most Romanians were happy to see Coca-Cola move in. Jobs were created by Coke and by other businesses that sprang up to support its sales and distribution. Romanians liked the quality of Coca-Cola products and were happy to learn new business skills.

Colgate-Palmolive entered the Romanian marketplace in late 1991, when it purchased controlling shares of the state-owned manufacturers of soap and personal-care products. Never before had Romanians had a choice of soaps to buy, but Colgate-Palmolive offered two brands. Romanians quickly became educated consumers who shopped for quality and value. Since then, several local brands of soap and toothpaste have been launched by Romanians, and the industry is doing well.

### International Investment

Romania's economic problems make many foreign businesses leery of investing heavily in the country. Legal issues complicate foreign investment as well, but the government is working to change that by enacting laws that give businesses the kinds of protection they receive in most other capitalist countries.

An influx of foreign money is exactly what could boost Romania's economy. Some international businesses have taken that step: Germany, South Korea, Italy, and the United States are the largest investors. Coca-Cola, McDonalds, Pizza Hut, Oracle, Proctor & Gamble, Amoco, Colgate-Palmolive,

Citibank, and IBM have all invested in Romania, as have many other small- and medium-sized American businesses. But the level of foreign investment is still disappointing to most Romanians.

## Agriculture

For centuries, agriculture has been a cornerstone of the Romanian economy. About 45 percent of the country's population live in rural areas, where most are engaged in some form of agriculture. Much of the food produced is used to feed Romanians, but the country also exports foods to other nations in Eastern Europe.

The breadbasket of Romania is Walachia, which provides half the annual grain harvest and roughly half the fruit, but other regions make important contributions, too. Corn, potatoes, and wheat are the main crops and staples of the

Harvesting potatoes

## What Romania Grows, Makes, and Mines

| Agriculture | |
|---|---|
| Corn | 10,000,000 metric tons |
| Potatoes | 3,200,000 metric tons |
| Wheat | 3,170,000 metric tons |
| **Manufacturing** | |
| Cement | 6,000,000 metric tons |
| Steel | 5,800,000 metric tons |
| Pig iron | 3,500,000 metric tons |
| **Mining** | |
| Coal | 40,550,000 metric tons |
| Iron | 180,000 metric tons |
| Bauxite | 174,000 metric tons |

**Tomatoes and corn grow on the Danube Delta.**

Romanian diet. Other crops include barley, oats, rice, sugar beets, soybeans, tobacco, and rye. Sunflowers and tomatoes grow well in the Danube Delta and elsewhere throughout the country. Wine grapes and table grapes are widely grown—the best vineyards are in Moldavia.

## Tourism

Romanians are also hoping that tourism will boost their economy. Foreign travelers find much to enjoy: Black Sea resorts and health spas in the Carpathians, as well as great scenery and skiing. Some tourists like to learn about

Romania's history and visit its many castles and museums, while others come to appreciate the fine folk art found in rural areas. The country currently attracts about 5.9 million tourists each year.

The problem for tourists comes when they need a place to eat and sleep. Few restaurants or hotels offer the quality of dining and accommodations that many world travelers have come to expect.

Tourists at a lakeside resort

## Hope is Fading

Romanians must put several pieces of the puzzle into place as they work to get their economy back in order. In the meantime, the people who were once so optimistic about their future are starting to feel hopelessness settle in. They struggle day to day to pay high prices for the things they need, while few jobs pay well. And constantly, the promise of a better tomorrow is broken.

President Constantinescu admits to tough challenges. In a 1998 speech to the U.S. Congress, he said, "We have learned that despite our profound and unflinching commitment to privatization and economic reform, it will be more difficult to rebuild the Romanian economy than we or our friends had expected."

# The People
# of Romania

84

ROMANIA HAS LITTLE OF THE OBVIOUS ETHNIC DIVERSITY we see in the United States and Canada. Of the country's 22.4 million residents, native Romanians make up the vast majority. People of Hungarian ancestry comprise the largest minority. Roma—once known as Gypsies—, Germans, and Ukrainians are other minorities. There is very little difference in the general physical appearance of these ethnic groups.

| Who Lives in Romania? | |
| --- | --- |
| Romanians | 89% |
| Hungarians | 9% |
| Roma, Germans, and Ukranians | 2% |

## Ethnic Unrest

Following World War II and through Ceauşescu's reign, the oppressive communist leadership in Romania left the residents

*Opposite:* **A young Romanian girl**

little room to express their ethnic individuality, so there was little ethnic unrest. The greater freedom of expression now available to Romanians allows more opportunity for troubles among peoples of differing backgrounds.

This has been seen most clearly in Transylvania, where most of the country's Hungarian residents live. Though Hungarians make up only about 9 percent of Romania's overall population, they make up about 30 percent of the population in Transylvania.

Under communist rule, the Romanian government worked hard to limit contact between Hungarians living in Hungary and those living in Transylvania. They wanted to make sure the Hungarians in Romania did not get any outside support. Hungarian newspapers and magazines were not allowed into Romania, and radio and television broadcasts from Hungary were closely monitored. Government agents even kept track of phone calls between Romania and Hungary.

After the communist rulers were overthrown in 1989, the Hungarians had more freedom to assert their rights. In 1990, Hungarians led a protest in the Transylvanian town of Tîrgu Mureş calling for greater use of Magyar, the Hungarian language, in schools and on printed government materials, including street signs. They were opposed by Romanian extremists who supported the use of violence to keep outside influences out of Romania. These extremists wanted to keep the Hungarians down, so fighting and riots broke out. Five people died.

Romanian extremists in Transylvania continued to call for further crackdown on the Hungarians. Many bilingual street signs were removed, and some church-sponsored Hungarian schools were closed.

In recent years, however, the government has attempted to ease tensions with the Hungarians in Romania. Bilingual street signs, for example, are allowed in areas that have a greater than

## The Holocaust

Before World War II, the Jewish population in Romania was the third largest in Europe—800,000 in 1939. The Holocaust had a lasting, horrifying effect on the ethnic make-up of Romania. When the war ended, only half of Romania's Jews remained. Some had left the country safely, but many more died.

Most Romanian Jews were not sent to the Nazi concentration camps—the government resisted this—but thousands were killed in massacres led by the Iron Guard, police, and Romanian soldiers, particularly in Moldavia and Bukovina. More than 100,000 Jews from these regions were marched into Romanian concentration camps. Amidst the cold and desolation, most died of sickness and starvation. In all, about 260,000 Romanian Jews were killed or died in the camps.

During World War II, Northern Transylvania was held by Hungary. About 120,000 of the region's 150,000 Jews were sent by the Nazis to concentration camps where many perished.

In Ceauşescu's reign, Jews were allowed to leave Romania for Israel after paying large sums of money. Many did. Today, the number of Jews in Romania is slightly less than 10,000, while Romanians make up one of the largest groups of foreign-born Israeli citizens.

30 percent Hungarian population. The government's Council for Ethnic Minorities helps to provide news for Hungarians and other minorities by subsidizing the translation of news reports into the native languages of minorities living in Romania. Some Hungarian-language daily newspapers are popular enough to survive without government subsidies. Several cable stations broadcast in the native languages of the ethnic minorities.

## Roma

The Roma people—once known as Gypsies—also suffered ethnic persecution in Romania following the fall of Ceauşescu. Roma are the descendants of people who came to Europe nearly 1,000 years ago from the regions around India and Iran. In the early 1800s, many Roma were kept as slaves by wealthy Romanians. They were freed only after a law emancipated them in 1848. Official population counts state that about 400,000 Roma live in Romania today, but other estimates place the actual number closer to 2 million. It is hard to get an exact count of the Roma population because they are nomadic

Roma children gather in a village.

people, moving from place to place as they look for work and the resources they need to survive. Usually, they travel in groups and set up camp in rural areas.

In general, the Roma are faced with widespread distrust and racist discrimination, and many people consider them criminals. They are often tormented by local officials and the police, making it difficult for them to get jobs and earn an honest living. When they are attacked and the violence results in injury or death, the blame usually falls on the Roma, whether or not they started the battle. Roma leaders approached the Romanian government in 1994 with a request for greater human rights, and they are working to change the impression that many people hold of them. The government responded with a series of programs, including caravan classrooms that will follow the Roma and provide education for the children and stricter law enforcement against those who harass Roma.

### Population Growth

The country's population has grown steadily, if rather slowly. In 1869, Romania's population was 8.9 million; in 1900, it was 11.1 million; in 1930, 14.3 million; in 1948, 15.8 million; and in 1989, 23.2 million. It is 22.4 million today.

| Population of Major Cities | |
|---|---|
| Bucharest | 2,400,000 |
| Constanţa | 349,000 |
| Iaşi | 340,000 |
| Timişoara | 328,000 |
| Cluj-Napoca | 326,000 |
| Galaţi | 326,000 |
| Braşov | 324,000 |

Population distribution in Romania

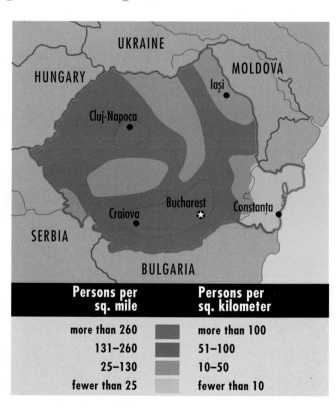

| Persons per sq. mile | | Persons per sq. kilometer |
|---|---|---|
| more than 260 | | more than 100 |
| 131–260 | | 51–100 |
| 25–130 | | 10–50 |
| fewer than 25 | | fewer than 10 |

This relatively slow population growth is caused by many factors. The region's poverty resulted in poor health care, so more babies and young children have died of sickness in Romania than elsewhere, and adults didn't live as long either. Thousands of people left the country during World War II and afterward, when the Soviets were in control. And, of course, hundreds of thousands of Romanian Jews and soldiers died in the war.

Romanians also put off having children. Following World War II, one benefit of communist rule was that education became more accessible. Young people postponed having families so that they could get more schooling. Women were

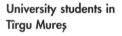

University students in
Tîrgu Mureș

**Apartment buildings in Galaţi**

encouraged to enter the work-force to help the nation's industrial growth. Their busy lives left little room for children, and neither did the small, cramped apartments common in urban Romania.

In 1965, when Nicolae Ceauşescu became president, he was disturbed by a population growth rate that was nearly zero. So few children were being born, he feared that there would not be enough workers. New laws were quickly passed. Abortion was outlawed and contraceptives were banned. Men and women who were childless after the age of twenty-five, married or not, were forced to pay heavy taxes. The government offered financial help to families with three or more children.

But the financial help was not enough to make it easy to raise a large family, and many women turned to illegal abortions. In the late 1980s, Romania's population was about 23 million. Ceauşescu's goal was to reach a national population of 30 million by 2000. It was a woman's "patriotic duty," he said, to give birth to many children. Even single women were strongly encouraged to have babies.

Had Ceauşescu remained in power, perhaps his goal would have been achieved. But his reign ended in 1989, and so did his policies. Though the population has climbed slightly from the late 1980s, the current figure falls far short of Ceauşescu's goal.

## Romanian Orphanages

Under Ceauşescu's law, thousands of unwanted children were born and many were abandoned in overcrowded, understaffed orphanages. The horrors that went on in some of them were nearly unimaginable. The children slept on beds of rags tossed over old pieces of linoleum. Some of them, especially those with disabilities, were tied with their arms and legs behind their backs, to make it easier for the workers to move them around, and to keep them from wandering. They were left that way for years at a time.

More children never made it to orphanages—they were abandoned to the street and have stayed there, begging for food and seeking shelter anywhere they can find a quiet spot. Some have formed communities of sorts in underground tunnels housing urban pipes and plumbing. There is no official count of homeless children living in the streets of Romania, but a

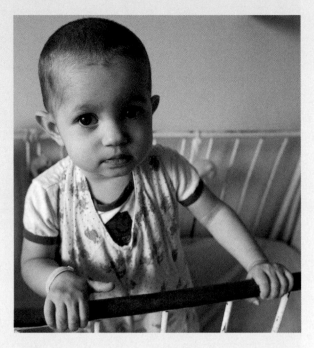

1998 estimate put the number at about 4,300, mostly in Bucharest.

Today, nearly 100,000 Romanian children live in institutions of some sort. Thousands more were adopted by foreigners in the first eighteen months following the world's discovery of the orphanage horrors in late 1989. But the government stopped most foreign adoptions in July 1991, supposedly to prevent the sale of babies. Since then, only a few international adoptions have been approved by the government.

## Language

As the name *Romania* came from the Romans who settled in the region about 2,000 years ago, so did the language. Most of the Roman troops and settlers who conquered Romania spoke a form of Latin, and this became the official language of their regional government. During their rule, Latin spread throughout the land. This common language helped to unify the people throughout the many years of foreign rule and national breakups they endured throughout the following centuries.

Romanian is a Romance language, based on Latin. It is spoken primarily in Romania and Moldova. Romanian also includes influences from other Romance languages such as French, Spanish, Italian, and Portuguese. Because Romania is surrounded by Slavic nations, there is a Slavic influence on the language as well, making it quite different from other Latin-based languages.

Many Romanians speak French as a second language. German is also commonly spoken and is helpful in international trade. In Transylvania, Hungarian is a more common second language because Hungary has at times controlled the area.

### Spelling Romania

There is some dispute over the correct spelling of the name *Romania*. In much of Europe, it is spelled *Rumania*, and this spelling is sometimes used in North America, too. But most Romanians prefer the spelling with an "o," to associate them with their Roman ancestors. The correct spelling of many words in the Romanian language today, in fact, is in dispute.

Communist rulers adopted laws in 1953 that stressed the Slavic origins of many words, and their spellings were changed to reflect this. Since 1989, however, many people have returned to the earlier spellings, and some confusion has arisen because both spellings can be found in printed materials throughout the country.

# A Nation of Believers

94

R OMANIANS ARE DEEPLY RELIGIOUS, BUT FOR MANY years under communist rule, they were prohibited from freely expressing their faith. Atheism—the denial that God exists—was declared the official belief of the nation. The Soviet Communists believed that religion would soon be replaced around the world as scientific knowledge grew.

The government did allow some religious practices to continue, however, to avoid massive protests. And the Romanian people took every possible advantage of this small bit of religious freedom. They marked weddings and funerals with religious ceremonies, and most babies were baptized. Families still celebrated Easter. Since the end of communist rule, restrictions have been lifted. Today, Romanians are free to worship as they wish. Nearly all Romanians are Christians.

### Early Christianity in Romania

When the land that is now Romania was still known as Dacia, ruled by the Roman Empire, Christianity was introduced, around the year A.D. 300. Followers placed their faith in the words of the Bible and in the teachings of Jesus Christ. Services were held in the Slavic language. In the

*Opposite:* **A nun carrying flowers outside a monastery**

| Romania's Major Religions | |
| --- | --- |
| Romanian Orthodox | 86% |
| Roman Catholic | 5% |
| Other (includes atheists) | 9% |

**A stone church in Moldavia**

year 1054, a split in the Christian Church divided it into the Eastern Orthodox Church and the Roman Catholic Church—and later, beginning in the 1500s, the Protestant religions. In Romania, the Eastern Orthodox Church took hold, and the Slavic language remained the norm for religious practice.

In the seventeenth century, however, the Romanian language began to be used for religious services. This was the beginning of the Romanian Orthodox Church. During the turbulent centuries that followed, when Romania was ruled by several countries and often divided among foreign rulers, the Romanian Orthodox Church provided a sense of unity that eventually helped to bring the nation together again.

### The Romanian Orthodox Church

The Romanian Orthodox Church is an independent segment of the Eastern Orthodox Church, headed by a patriarch in Bucharest. Teachings are based on the Bible and on the holy traditions of the Church, set in place by the apostles—followers of Christ on earth. According to Romanian Orthodoxy, the apostles were infallible—free from error—but no one man can be infallible. For this reason, they do not accept the infallibility of the pope.

The Church is led by bishops, priests, and deacons. Bishops and those priests and deacons living in monasteries are not allowed to marry, but priests and deacons who serve parishes may be married if their weddings took place before their ordinations.

## Andrei Şaguna

Andrei Şaguna was an outstanding leader in the Romanian Orthodox Church. Born in 1809, he completed his religious studies in Serbia and became a monk in 1833. After settling in Transylvania, his dynamic personality allowed him to climb through the ranks and he became a bishop in 1848. Şaguna was a strong defender of the rights of Romanians who worked to promote better education for all, along with literature and culture. In 1864, he was promoted to the role of metropolitan—a top leader in the Church. He reorganized the Romanian Orthodox Church and made it an activist force for the rights of all Romanians.

## Bukovina's Painted Monasteries

The walls of many fifteenth- and sixteenth-century monasteries in Bukovina are decorated with beautiful frescoes. These religious paintings served to remind passersby of God and Bible stories. Even people who couldn't read could understand the stories through pictures. In a way, the frescoes might be considered the world's first billboards.

Sometimes political feelings are expressed, too, as in the frescoes on the Voroneţ Monastery, in which doomed souls heading to hell are shown wearing turbans like those worn by the Ottoman Turks who invaded Romania. The angels overhead carry trumpets that look just like the horns carried by local shepherds.

A mystery still surrounds the ingredients used to paint these frescoes, which have endured so well over the centuries. No records were left behind, so scientists from some of the world's leading universities, including the Massachusetts Institute of Technology, have traveled to Romania in an effort to discover what the paint was made of. Thus far, they've identified about thirty ingredients, including honey, vinegar, and egg; there are still about ten more unknown substances in the mix.

*Above left:* **Orthodox churches are beautifully decorated.**

*Above right:* **A woman leaving an Orthodox church**

Members of the Romanian Orthodox Church worship in beautifully decorated churches filled with icons—religious images. In each church, the altar is at the front in the center of the sanctuary, separated from worshipers by a screen called an *iconostasis*. The congregation watches the service through openings in the iconostasis.

Some of the most prominent icons in Romanian Orthodox churches depict Mary, the mother of Jesus, who is deeply loved and revered. All saints are honored and prayed to, because the Romanian Orthodox Church believes that saints will take their prayers directly to God. Many Romanian Orthodox families also keep icons in their homes.

There are seven holy sacraments—rites—of the Romanian Orthodox Church. The first of these is baptism. Immediately following baptism, the second sacrament—confirmation—is performed, giving the individual complete church membership, including the right to take part in the Eucharist.

A priest performing a holy sacrament

The Eucharist is a remembrance of Jesus Christ rising from the dead after his crucifixion. Members of the Church share bread and wine that they believe has been transformed into the body and blood of Christ by the Holy Spirit. In confession, a person admits his or her sins to God, before a priest, and receives forgiveness.

Marriage is another holy sacrament, but divorce is allowed. In fact, three marriages are permitted, but the first is considered to be the most important in the eyes of God.

Holy Orders is a sacrament in which men take the vows to become priests and deacons. This can only be administered by a bishop, and members of the parish take part in the ceremony.

The final sacrament is the anointing of the sick. A priest offers this sacrament to a seriously ill person, praying for healing and forgiveness.

### The Pope Visits Romania

Pope John Paul II made a three-day visit to Romania in May 1999, the first papal visit in nearly 1,000 years to a nation of mostly Orthodox Church members. The pope was greeted by the head of the Romanian Orthodox Church, Patriarch Teoctist. He met with President Constantinescu, led a Catholic mass, and attended an Orthodox Church service. The pope and patriarch were both optimistic that their meeting could help to heal the divisions between their churches. Though most Romanian Catholics live in the Transylvania region, the pope remained in Bucharest. Several hundred thousand Catholics traveled on special trains to see the pope, and many more rural citizens made difficult journeys just to get to a television set to view the papal visit.

## Catholicism

The Roman Catholic Church is similar to the Romanian Orthodox Church, but there are a few major differences. One difference is that Roman Catholics believe that the pope is the supreme authority in the Church.

Roman Catholics receive the same sacraments as Romanian Orthodox Church members do, but Roman Catholic infants receive only baptism and must wait until they are older for the Eucharist and confirmation. Roman Catholics may marry only once, and priests cannot be married.

## Other Religions

A variety of world religions are also practiced in Romania, including Reformed Lutheran, Greek Orthodox, Pentecostal, and Islam, as well as Baptist, Judaism, and Unitarian. Most of the country's Roman Catholics and Lutherans are ethnic Hungarians or Germans. The majority of the Muslims are ethnic Turks and Tatars living in the Dobrogea region.

The Eastern Orthodox Church, also known as the Uniate Church, is favored by ethnic Romanians in Transylvania. Created in 1699, this church combines the key principles of Orthodox Christianity and Roman Catholicism. While Uniates follow Orthodox rituals, they also accept the authority of the pope and some other Catholic principles. Communists forced this Church to unite with the Romanian Orthodox Church during their years in power, but the two churches split again after 1989.

CHAPTER

NINE

# Artists and Athletes

102

THE ARTS HAVE FLOURISHED IN ROMANIA, EVEN THOUGH its people have so often been repressed by foreign rulers and suffered economic hardship. These circumstances have not stifled the creative energies of its artists or held back the country's great athletes. The people take great pride in this and relish the accomplishments of their fellow Romanians.

*Opposite:* **Wooden spoons carved by an artist**

## Artists

A quick tour through nearly any part of the Romanian countryside shows the artistic nature of Romanians. Houses, though modest, are often adorned with brilliant, colorful paintings and intricate wood carvings. Doorways are decorated

**A brightly painted house**

to welcome visitors. Clothing, too, has an artistic touch—colorful, traditional peasant costumes are still worn by some people on Sundays and for weddings and festivals.

Folk art is plentiful throughout Romania, particularly in the countryside. Beautifully decorated eggs are showcased at Easter, and lovely pottery and ornaments are common in homes year-round. Even tools sometimes get a special touch—a bit of carving or painting on the handle. Techniques for these handicrafts are usually passed down from generation to generation. Girls learn from their mothers; boys, from their fathers.

Romania's most famous artist is sculptor Constantin Brâncuşi, who lived from 1876 to 1957. As a youngster, he was a shepherd in the Carpathian Mountains. He learned his sculpting techniques as a boy, watching the men of his village carve designs into the wooden rafters and doorways of local homes and churches. Though he left Romania for Paris while in his twenties, Brâncuşi continued to draw on the folk art and mythology of his youth for inspiration. He worked those ideas into modern abstract art that is prized worldwide. Most of his pieces are on

**"Sleep," by Constantin Brâncuşi**

display in the United States and France, but a sculpture garden near his hometown also showcases his work.

## Literature

Romanian folklore is grand—stories of terrible hardships, tales of great heroism, nearly larger than life. Folklore was originally passed down through oral tradition, as each generation told the tales to the next generation. This helped to remind people of their history, their shared values, and their common bonds. Romania's folklore has continued into modern times, reflected in its literature, poetry, and drama.

In the late 1600s, Miron Costin wrote a historical account of Moldavia. His work and that of others traced the history and culture of Romanians in a new way and inspired readers to think of themselves as an ethnic group with its own identity. Costin's son, Nicolae, was one of the first people to gather folklore and legends of the area and write them down, adding to the emerging cultural identity of Romanians.

The centuries that followed saw a rise in the popularity of poetry and literature based on romance, war, history, and religion. Many Romanian writers took on these themes. Their works helped to keep alive the common bonds among Romanians, just as the oral folklore had done before.

Playwright Eugene Ionesco credited his thirteen years living in Romania during fascist rule with giving much of the shape to his creations. In the 1950s, he became world renowned for his work in what is called "theater of the absurd"—surreal writing that incorporates tragedy and comedy.

## Dracula

The book that brought perhaps the most fame to Romania was not written by a Romanian at all—in fact, its Irish author never even visited the Transylvania region in which his story is based. The book was Bram Stoker's *Dracula*, written in 1897. It took a true story from Romanian history and expanded it into one of the world's most famous tales of horror.

The true story is this: Vlad IV, born in 1431, was the son of a fierce Walachian soldier and statesman nicknamed *Dracul*, or "the Devil." As a teenager, Vlad was imprisoned by the Turks for five years, a period that shaped his personality, training him in fighting and terror. After gaining his freedom, he became a fearsome ruler of Walachia in 1456.

Crime was nearly wiped out during his reign, as he punished even minor thefts with death. Criminals were impaled—killed by stakes pounded through their bodies—in a public area for all to see. Vlad also got rid of poverty in his own way. He invited the poor and disabled of Walachia to join him at a dinner, and asked if they wished to be free of their suffering. When they said "yes," he had them all killed. He became known as *Dracula*, or "son of the Devil," after his father. He was also called *Vlad Țepeș*, "The Impaler."

If he was this harsh with his own people, it's not hard to imagine how terrifying a warrior Vlad was.

After winning against the Saxons, he held a celebration in a garden decorated with the impaled bodies of his victims. Another time, a Turkish army was greeted by a field full of the impaled bodies of 20,000 of their fellow Turks. They immediately turned around. During his reign, Vlad had about 100,000 people impaled.

The Turks put an end to Dracula in 1476 though. They cut off his head and presented it to their leader. The rest of his body was buried at the Snagov Monastery. Nothing was inscribed on his tomb, and it remains that way today.

Some 400 years later, Bram Stoker mixed the tales he'd heard of Dracula with folklore of bloodsucking vampires. Today, Transylvania is known around the world as Dracula's home, even though most of the story is more fiction than fact. Tour guides lead visitors to Bran Castle, an eerie building with towers and turrets, high in the Transylvanian mountains. Though Vlad Țepeș only visited there, it looks like his legendary home. Among its true inhabitants was the beloved Queen Marie.

Poet Mihai Eminescu, born in 1850 in northern Moldavia, created a school of poetry that influenced Romanian writers of the nineteenth and twentieth centuries. He was noted for his insight into the social needs of the people. He used his prominence as a writer to focus concern on the problems of peasants, whom he felt were the true Romanians. Many people feel that his work represents the idealistic soul of Romania. It focuses on personal courage in the face of great failure and disappointment in life. He is considered the country's national poet.

**Romania's national poet, Mihai Eminescu**

Women, too, have left their marks on Romania's literary pages. Magda Isanos wrote many beloved poems, even though she died when she was only twenty-eight. Born in 1916, she grew up in Moldavia and published her first poetry while still in high school. Her works were loved because they approached tragedy with optimism, something so meaningful to Romanians.

Folk music has been part of Romanian culture for centuries, passed down from generation to generation. It is still performed regularly today, at festivals and on holidays, at weddings and funerals. Rhythms, tunes, and instruments are different around the country. In the Carpathians, folk instruments include panpipes and a long wooden horn called a bacium. These are common among shepherds who guard animal flocks on the hillsides. Music from the area between Moldavia and Transylvania is played on a violin and

**A folk violinist in Transylvania**

a *gardon*—a stringed instrument shaped like a large violin and played by hitting a stick on the strings.

Song, in Romanian folk music, is an important way of telling a story or expressing an emotion. Ballads and epic songs are especially important in the southern regions of Romania. Some songs are about great warriors; other tell grand love stories. The doină is a sort of poetic song that expresses the sorrowful emotions of the singer. These songs may be improvised as the singer goes along. Roma bands are fond of playing this sort of tune.

Internationally-known composer and violinist Georges Enesco was born near Dorohoi in 1881. Also a pianist and a conductor, he drew on his Romanian heritage in his work, incorporating melodies from Roma tunes into his music. He wrote three symphonies, an opera, and *Romanian Rhapsodies*, based on folk tunes. Every three years, a music festival is held in his honor in Bucharest. Enesco died in 1955.

Today, popular culture in Romania is being influenced more and more by the international media. Western music, such as rock, disco, and jazz, is popular with younger Romanians, and folk music is fading into history.

## Weddings and Funerals

Lengthy rituals invoking the country's colorful artistic history surround traditional weddings and funerals in Romania. Most of these customs have been left behind in urban areas, but they remain in many rural areas.

Weddings take place on Sundays, after several days of events leading up to the main ceremony. Parents of the bride and groom are honored. Their children formally ask them for forgiveness for leaving the family fold. Advice, often in the form of poetry, is

offered up to the young couple. Special bread is baked for them to share during the marriage ceremony.

When the big day arrives, bridesmaids assist the bride as she braids her hair and adorns it with a headband covered in colorful jewels, flowers, and ribbons. Best men help the groom prepare. He shaves his beard, symbolizing the end of his bachelor days. He wears a special goatskin vest. During the wedding, his best man carries a pole covered with handkerchiefs and bells.

A band of fiddlers usually accompanies the groom and his group to the church, sometimes stopping off along the way at the home of the bride. They play while she sings an emotional farewell to her family, friends, and single life. The music goes on long after the wedding, with dancing and partying. Usually, the bride takes turns dancing with the guests, who offer her money.

Funerals, too, take on great symbolism, particularly in northern Transylvania, where the rituals are elaborate. Many people there believe that if any step in the lengthy funeral routine is missed, the soul of the dead may come back as a ghost. The deceased lies for three days in his or her former home as neighbors come to pay their respects; during this time, church bells ring three times a day. On the third day, the priest arrives at the home. He etches a cross on a wall that must remain for a full year. The coffin is carried through the town to the church. Following a brief funeral, everyone throws a handful of dirt into the grave, and special bread symbolizing Christ's victory over death is handed out. Special meals are shared three days later, and again after nine days, six weeks, and six months. After one year of mourning, a feast is given for the surviving family members.

## Award-Winning Museums

Opened to the public in 1991, the Cotrenci Palace is one of Romania's newest museums, but the palace itself dates back to 1893. It was built on the site of an earlier palace, constructed in 1679, that housed Romanian princes for more than 200 years. The museum contains a collection of furniture, glassware, pottery, textiles, and other decorative items that give visitors a glimpse into the luxurious lives of Romanian royalty in the early twentieth century. The Cotrenci Palace received the European Museum of the Year Award in 1994.

Two years later, that award went to another Bucharest museum, the Museum of the Romanian Peasant. More than 90,000 items here preserve the rich peasant traditions that are so much a part of Romania's history. The collection includes centuries-old pottery, traditional costumes, and carved wooden furniture and tools. The museum has even acquired six wooden churches. Four are being preserved in their original locations, but two were actually moved right into the museum.

## Movies

Beginning in the early 1900s, artists used film to tell stories of brave individuals struggling for their rights while oppressed by evil rulers. This theme runs through so much of Romania's art because it represents the lives of the Romanian people. That same oppression eventually took hold of the film industry.

In the 1970s and 1980s, the government censored movies, allowing nothing that seemed to criticize the rulers. But many filmmakers continued to make films in which their antigovernment messages were hidden within the story—there were codes in which certain simple characters represented deeper themes. These were called "iceberg movies" because, like icebergs, much of their substance was hidden below the surface. Today, the film industry is enjoying artistic freedom, although financial problems within Romania have caused struggles for filmmakers, as they have for so many others.

## Sports

Romanians take pride in their athletic ability, and many have achieved success in such varied sports as basketball and tennis. But in terms of sports, Romania is perhaps best known around the world for its great gymnasts. Girls and boys learn

Romania's women's gymnastics team won the world championship in 1999.

the sport at a young age, and those with particular talent are placed in special government-run programs. The women's national team is always a force in world competition—in 1995 and 1999, it won the world championship.

Among most Romanians, though, nothing is more popular than soccer. In 1994, the Romanian soccer team made it to the quarterfinals in the World Cup. The excitement energized the nation and encouraged more soccer players than ever before. Children and adults around the country play on local teams.

## Famous Sports Stars

Nadia Comaneci may be Romania's best-known athlete. When she was fourteen, she earned seven perfect scores in the gymnastics competition at the 1976 Summer Olympics in Montreal, Canada. No one had ever earned such high marks. She won three gold medals and became the Olympic all-around champion.

Comaneci started gymnastics training at age six with coach Bela Karolyi, an ethnic Hungarian. After the 1976 Olympics, she continued to compete at many international competitions, and she earned two more gold medals and a silver at the 1980 Olympic Games held in Moscow. She retired from competition in 1981 and became a government gymnastics coach. Karolyi went on to train several more Olympians, including Mary Lou Retton and Dominique Moceanu, an American whose parents came from Romania.

### Gheorghe Mureşan

At 7 feet 7 inches (231 cm) tall, Gheorghe Mureşan gets noticed, even on the NBA basketball courts where he plays with the New Jersey Nets. Mureşan, the tallest player ever, comes by his size because of a pituitary gland condition—not from genetics. Mureşan was born in 1971 in Tritenii, Transylvania, and attended nearby Cluj University. He began playing basketball at age fourteen when he was recruited by his dentist, who also treated the national basketball team. He played for the Romanian national team and a French team before moving to the United States in 1993. Following the 1995–1996 season, he was selected as the most improved player in the NBA. In 1998, he costarred with Billy Crystal in the movie *My Giant*.

Comaneci stunned the world when she left Romania in 1989, drawing attention to the harsh life Romanians suffered under Nicolae Ceauşescu. Today, she is married to another former Olympic gymnast, Bart Conner. They live in Oklahoma and run a gymnastics academy.

Ilie Nastase was the first Romanian tennis player to gain international fame. He was among the world's top players from 1971 to 1975, but his career actually spanned twenty-six years, during which he won fifty-seven singles tennis titles. He showed an interest in politics after retiring, but lost a 1996 election for mayor of Bucharest.

Nastase's doubles tennis partner, Ion Tiriac, never achieved the same stardom as Nastase, but he is well respected in Romania today for his work after leaving tennis. He has promoted foreign investment in the country, he owns the Ion Tiriac Commercial Bank, and he established a school for orphans in Braşov, his hometown.

**Ilie Nastase playing at an AIDS benefit in 1994**

# Lives of Hope

EDUCATION IS VALUED IN ROMANIA. THE NATION BOASTS many universities and technical institutes, and there is almost no illiteracy. Schooling is free and compulsory.

Romanians see education as a way to move up in life—to a better job, a nicer home, an easier life. Sometimes this happens, but often it doesn't. Still, education is prized for the ability it gives people to understand and appreciate the world around them.

*Opposite:* **Folk dancers at a festival**

**The University of Bucharest**

The many festivals in Romania provide another way of interpreting life and the world. Some are based in religious beliefs, while others celebrate the seasons and the harvests. Some are celebrated nationwide, but many communities have their own unique celebrations.

Christmas and Easter are two of the main religious holidays in Romania. Christmas preparations begin on Saint Nicholas Day, December 6, when families feast on freshly slaughtered animals. On Christmas Eve, groups go from door to door singing the *colinde*—songs wishing health and prosperity for the coming year. They exchange pastries called *turte*, made of thin layers of dough to represent the swaddling clothes wrapped around Baby Jesus. The feasting and dancing often go on for days.

Easter is the most important religious feast. Ceremonies begin a week earlier, on Palm Sunday. The following week is solemn, particularly Good Friday, which commemorates the death of Christ, but on Easter Sunday, believers rejoice that he rose from the dead.

**A candlelit Easter gathering**

On New Year's Day, capras dance through the streets in Moldavia.

New Year's Day is time for another happy celebration. In some parts of the country, a plow is dragged from home to home. Decorated in green leaves to represent growth and fertility in the new year, it is supposed to bring good luck to each home it visits. In Moldavia, a *capra*—a man dressed in red and black and wearing a goat's-head mask—dances wildly through the streets, accompanied by the music of flutes and drums.

## Holidays in Romania

| | |
|---|---|
| New Year's Day | January 1 |
| Palm Sunday | A Sunday in spring (date varies) |
| Easter | The Sunday after Palm Sunday |
| Labor Day | May 1 and 2 |
| National Day | December 1 |
| Christmas | December 25 |

In Braşov, in Transylvania, the pageant of *Juni* is held each year on the first Sunday of May. The festival features young men of the community dressed in fancy costumes, parading through the city to the music of a brass band. Singing, dancing, and feasting into the night finish off the event.

Another Transylvanian festival celebrates young women. *Tîrgul de fete* (The Girl Fair) is a centuries-old tradition held in the town of Muntele Gâina in summer. At one time, it gave the young herdsmen of the area, who were away much of the year guarding their flocks of animals, an opportunity to meet possible mates. The young women dressed in their finest clothes and often brought along goods to display how generous their dowry, or marriage payment, would be. Today, this part of the festival is just a memory, but people still gather atop Mount Gaina to enjoy music, dancing, food, and drink.

In summer, many rural communities celebrate the festival of *sinzienele*, around the summer solstice. Each community has its own rituals, but all feature one event—*sinziene*, in which the women collect wild leaves, flowers, and roots. These herbs symbolize good luck, and they are also used for medicinal purposes in the coming year.

Harvest festivals are common in the summer and fall, kicking off in June with a Cherry Festival in the town of Brincovenesti. In earlier times, harvest festivals gave rural farmers a reason and opportunity to gather and share news. Today, people get together just for fun, forgetting their worries for a while.

Good food is an important part of Romanian celebrations, but many of Romania's most traditional foods aren't often prepared today. Most contain a good deal of meat, particularly pork, but also beef, lamb, and chicken. Today, with the country's poor economy, meat is harder to come by. Vegetarian dishes are more common, as are weak broths made with boiled pork or chicken bones, and filled out with a bit of rice. Many recipes use less expensive, less desirable cuts of meat, as well—organs such as liver, heart, and brain are found in some dishes.

## *Rakott Káposzta* (Layered Sauerkraut)

The most common meat in Romania is pork, prepared in many forms, and cabbage is the most popular vegetable. *Rakott Káposzta* (Layered Sauerkraut) contains both.

This old Transylvanian dish has been popular for centuries. One of the region's oldest books on food, written by Miklós Misztófalusy-Kis in 1695, contains a version of this recipe. It has been updated over time, as each generation makes its changes to accommodate foods available at the time.

### *Rakott Káposzta* (Layered Sauerkraut)
Ingredients:
    4 pounds sauerkraut
    3/4 cup rice, uncooked
    1 1/2 cups beef broth
    1 large onion, chopped
    1 1/2 pounds ground pork
    1 teaspoon paprika
    10 ounces smoked sausage, sliced
    1 cup sour cream
    1 cup heavy cream
    4 ounces bacon, diced and cooked

Preheat oven to 350 °F. Heat the sauerkraut in a pan, then drain off the juice and set aside. In another pan, heat the broth to boiling, add the rice, and cover. Cook over low heat for 15 minutes, stirring occasionally. In a skillet, fry the ground pork along with the onion for about 15 minutes, until the pork is browned and the onion is softened. Remove from heat, drain off excess grease, and add the paprika. In a greased casserole dish, layer one-third of the hot sauerkraut, half the rice, half the pork mixture, and one-third of the sausage. Stir together the sour cream and heavy cream, and pour one-third of this mixture over the layers. Then make another layer just as above, and cover with the remaining sauerkraut. Place the remaining sausage and bacon over the sauerkraut, and top with the remaining sour cream mixture. Cover, and bake for about 20 minutes, until heated through.

Bread is a staple, as it has always been. Vegetables and fruits such as corn, cabbage, carrots, strawberries, and cherries are always appreciated.

Here are a few favorites from Romanian kitchens. *Ciorba* is soup made from the sour juice of fermented bran along with bacon, potatoes, and beef or chicken. Hearty stews are often accompanied by *mamaliga*, a baked cornmeal dish. *Sarmale* is a spicy dish of sour cabbage or grape leaves stuffed with meat and rice, and often served with sour cream. Sarmale shows a strong Greek influence. *Mititei* are small grilled sausages of pork, sometimes with beef or lamb added, seasoned with spicy herbs. In the large cities, these tasty sausages are often sold by street vendors.

**Sausages are a popular food.**

### Turkish Coffee

Coffee is a favorite beverage among Romanians. Usually, they drink it hot, strong, and sweetened, the way Romanians learned to drink it long ago, when invading Ottoman Turks brought coffee to the region. During that time, coffee was not taken with the rest of the meal. According to Turkish custom, people did not discuss topics such as war, politics, or taxes while eating. Only later, when the coffee was served, were such unpleasant subjects allowed. Many Romanian cities today have *patisseries*, where you can buy a cup of coffee and a small pastry or cake. Separate rooms for eating the sweet and drinking the coffee are usually provided. It's still hard to do both at once, because the Turkish custom lingers on.

When Romanians are thirsty, they enjoy drinking milk. The national alcoholic drink is a brandy, usually made from plums, called *tuica*. It's the traditional beverage at weddings and other festive occasions. Many fine wines are made in Romania, particularly the southeastern region, and people enjoy these, too.

## Clothing

Just as Romania's traditional foods are served less frequently these days, traditional clothing is now worn daily in only a few remote regions in the northern Carpathians. Elsewhere, it is worn for special occasions—weddings, festivals, and holidays. Most Romanians wear the same clothes as most people in the Western world—modern skirts, dresses, shirts, and slacks. Blue jeans are popular with young people.

The traditional outfits are beautiful, bright, and decorative. They were often handmade by peasant women who spun and wove the fabric from wool, flax, cotton, or silk and embroidered intricate designs onto white blouses with threads

**Children in colorful traditional costumes**

of gold, red, and black. Skirts are covered by colorful aprons, usually featuring geometric prints and stripes. Scarves complete the outfit. Traditional clothing for men usually consists of a plain white shirt, cinched at the waist with a leather belt or a colorful woven sash, worn over plain white pants. They wear hats of straw, felt, or lambskin, depending on the weather; and vests or jackets of sheepskin, leather, or richly embroidered fabric.

## Homes

Most urban Romanians live in small houses and apartments. The rural homes of Romanian peasants are typically painted in bright colors and adorned with intricate wood carvings with front porches and flower-filled yards. Inside, wooden furniture is decorated with carvings, and the women's embroidery is seen in curtains, tablecloths, and other linens. Backyards usually contain a few smaller buildings to store wood for winter fuel and food for livestock.

**A peasant family at home**

### Oina

Oina is a popular game for young people, played mostly in Romania's rural areas. Children gather into two teams on an open field, and the game starts when a ball is thrown by a player on one team and hit with a bat by an opposing player. It's somewhat like baseball, but there are no bases. A national tournament is held each year.

## Media

Romania has no lack of news publications, with several hundred weekly and daily newspapers, political magazines, and journals. Romanians also enjoy reading about culture, religion, and history in magazines focusing on these topics.

For many years, Romanians were able to watch only about two hours of television a day—all the programming that was made available by the Ceauşescu government. Today, the nation has about 70 television stations, and about 20 percent of the rural population and 80 percent of the urban population watch some television regularly. There are also more than 135 radio stations. Most of these media outlets have come onto the scene since 1990, when the censorship restrictions were lifted. Much more news reporting is available, and stations playing Western pop music are also popular.

## Transportation

Romanians get around in many ways. In rural areas, it's common to see carts pulled by an ox or a horse, while fancy, modern cars take to the streets in the urban centers. Walking is common everywhere, and buses and taxis are often used to get around in cities. Bicycles, however, are rare. In many rural areas, the terrain is too hilly and the roads are too poor for easy biking, and

Trams provide local transportation in Bucharest.

in many cities, the traffic is too heavy for safe cycling. For longer journeys, the country's largest cities have modern airports, but rail travel is far more common. Though many trains are poorly lit and chilly, train travel is cheap and usually efficient.

## Free Time

Romanians usually keep busy. Much of their free time is spent on such practical pursuits as home and car repair, growing food, and sewing clothes. But when they do take time out to relax, Romanians enjoy their free time in much the same way as people in North America. They like taking walks, going on family picnics, playing chess, listening to music, seeing movies, and watching television.

Romanians have experienced so much hardship that they are always trying to get ahead. With the hope that their government and economy are improving comes the hope for greater personal opportunities to exercise their characteristic optimism and love of life.

# Timeline

## Romanian History

| | |
|---|---|
| Stone Age dwellers live in Carpathian Mountain caves. | **4,000** B.C. |
| Dacians arrive in region that is Romania. | 800–300 B.C. |
| Romans conquer Dacians. | A.D.106 |
| Region became Roman province of Dacia. | 107 |
| Barbarians conquer Dacia. | 271 |
| Walachia, Moldavia, and Transylvania emerge as independent regions. | 1250–1350 |
| Turkish Ottomans advance into Walachia and Moldavia and take control. | 1400–1800 |
| Hungary loses control of Transylvania region to Turkish Ottomans. | 1526 |
| Romanian Orthodox Church begins. | 1600s |
| Wealthy Greeks, called Phanariots, rule Walachia and Moldavia. | 1700–1821 |
| Peasants revolt in Transylvania, and again in 1819 and throughout the 1840s. | 1784 |
| Transylvania made a part of Hungary. | 1848 |
| Moldavia and Walachia unite as Romania. Alexandru Ioan Cuza is made prince. | 1861 |
| Prince Alexandru Ioan Cuza is forced to abdicate. Prince Carol takes his place. | 1866 |
| Romanians declare independence. | 1877 |
| Ottoman Turks give up control of Romania. | 1878 |
| Romania becomes a kingdom. Prince Carol became King Carol I. | 1881 |

## World History

| | |
|---|---|
| 2500 B.C. | Egyptians build the Pyramids and Sphinx in Giza. |
| 563 B.C. | Buddha is born in India. |
| A.D. 313 | The Roman emperor Constantine recognizes Christianity. |
| 610 | The prophet Muhammad begins preaching a new religion called Islam. |
| 1054 | The Eastern (Orthodox) and Western (Roman) Churches break apart. |
| 1066 | William the Conqueror defeats the English in the Battle of Hastings. |
| 1095 | Pope Urban II proclaims the First Crusade. |
| 1215 | King John seals the Magna Carta. |
| 1300s | The Renaissance begins in Italy. |
| 1347 | The Black Death sweeps through Europe. |
| 1453 | Ottoman Turks capture Constantinople, conquering the Byzantine Empire. |
| 1492 | Columbus arrives in North America. |
| 1500s | The Reformation leads to the birth of Protestantism. |
| 1776 | The Declaration of Independence is signed. |
| 1789 | The French Revolution begins. |
| 1865 | The American Civil War ends. |

| Romanian History | | World History | |
|---|---|---|---|
| Peasants revolt in Romania. | **1888, 1907** | | |
| Romanian Army is involved in the second Balkan War. Bulgaria is forced to turn over the Dobrogea region to Romania. | **1913** | | |
| King Carol dies. Prince Ferdinand becomes King. | **1914** | **1914** | World War I breaks out. |
| Romania joins the war on the side of the Allies. Enemy troops from Bulgaria, Austria, and Hungary descend on Romania and take control. | **1916** | | |
| | | **1917** | The Bolshevik Revolution brings communism to Russia. |
| Treaty of Bucharest forces Romania to return Dobrogea to Bulgaria, and parts of the Carpathian Mountain region bordering Transylvania to Austria and Hungary. | **1918** | | |
| Romanians take Transylvania from Hungary. | **1918** | | |
| Romania acquires the Bukovina and Banat regions, and land to the north of Transylvania and east of Moldavia. | **1920** | | |
| King Ferdinand dies. Corneliu Codreanu, founder of the Iron Guard, provides leadership. | **1927** | | |
| King Carol II assumes the throne. | **1930** | **1929** | Worldwide economic depression begins. |
| Codreanu and many of his associates are imprisoned. | **1933** | | |
| Codreanu is killed. King Carol II declares a royal dictatorship. | **1938** | | |
| Romania joins WWII on side of Germany. King Carol gives up throne, his son Michael becomes king. | **1940** | **1939** | World War II begins, following the German invasion of Poland. |
| Romania changes sides, joins Allies in WWII. | **1944** | | |
| Communists become majority party in Romania, following national election. | **1946** | | |
| King Michael is forced off the throne. Romania is declared a People's Republic. | **1947** | | |
| Gheorghe Gheorghiu-Dej, head of the Romanian Communist Party, declares that Romania should be free of Soviet control. | **1962** | **1957** | The Vietnam War starts. |
| Gheorghiu-Dej dies. Nicolai Ceausescu becomes dictator. | **1965** | | |
| Nicolae Ceausescu and his wife, Elena, are executed. Ion Iliescu becomes interim president. | **1989** | **1989** | The Berlin Wall is torn down, as communism crumbles in Eastern Europe. |
| Iliescu elected president in national election. | **1990** | | |
| New Romanian constitution adopted. The nation is a parliamentary republic. | **1991** | | |
| Iliescu is reelected. | **1992** | | |
| Emil Constantinescu is elected president. | **1996** | **1996** | Bill Clinton is reelected U.S. president. |
| Pope John Paul II visits Romania. | **1999** | | |

# Fast Facts

**Official name:** Romania

**Capital:** Bucharest

**Official language:** Romanian

**Official religion:** None

Bucharest

Romania's flag

A mountain lake

| | |
|---|---|
| **Year of founding:** | 1989, as Romania in its present form |
| **National anthem:** | "Awaken Thee, Romanian," written for the 1848 Revolution by Romanian poet Andrei Mureşan |
| **Type of government:** | Republic |
| **Chief of state:** | President |
| **Head of government:** | Prime minister |
| **Area and dimensions of country:** | 91,699 square miles (237,482 sq km); approximately 450 miles (724 km) east to west and 320 miles (515 km) north to south It is halfway between the equator and the North Pole; and halfway between Europe's easternmost and westernmost points. |
| **Coordinates of geographic center:** | 46° 00′ N, 25° 00′ E |
| **Bordering countries:** | Ukraine to the north and east, Moldova to the east, Bulgaria to the south, Serbia to the southwest, and Hungary to the northwest |
| **Highest elevation:** | Mount Moldoveanu, 8,343 feet (2,543 m) above sea level |
| **Lowest elevation:** | Sea level, along the Black Sea coastline |
| **Average temperature extremes:** | The average temperature on the plains is 75° to 85° F (23.9° to 29.4° C). In the winters, the average temperature in the capital of Bucharest is 26° F (-3° C). |
| **Average precipitation:** | 50 inches (127 cm) or greater in the mountains, which is more than twice the amount on the plains |

A painted monastery

Currency

| National population: | 22,400,000 (est.) | |
| --- | --- | --- |
| **Population of largest cities:** | Bucharest | 2,400,000 |
| | Constanţa | 350,000 |
| | Iaşi | 340,000 |
| | Timişoara | 328,000 |
| | Cluj-Napoca | 326,000 |

**Famous landmarks:**
- ▶ *Bran Castle*, near Predeal in Transylvania
- ▶ *Cotrenci Palace Museum*, Bucharest
- ▶ *Mamaia Resort*, on the Black Sea coast near Constanţa
- ▶ *Painted Monasteries*, throughout southern Bukovina
- ▶ *People's Palace*, Bucharest
- ▶ *Retezat National Park*, in the southern Carpathians in Transylvania

**Industry:** An important part of Romanian industry is food production, both for feeding the country and for export. Other important consumer goods produced are clothing and textiles, shoes and leather goods, furniture, beer, and wine. Romania also manufactures simple machines and components for large machinery, fertilizer, cement, steel, pig iron, and aluminum.

**Currency:** Romania's basic unit of currency is the *leu* (plural *lei*) which means "lion" in Romanian. In June 2000, U.S.$1=20,815 lei.

**Weights and measures:** Metric system

**Literacy (1990 est.):** 97%

**Common Romanian words and phrases:**

| | |
| --- | --- |
| *da* | yes |
| *nu* | no |
| *vă rog* | please |
| *nultumesc* | thank you |

Taking a mud bath in the
Black Sea

Nadia Comaneci

| | |
|---|---|
| *Buna dimineata* | Good morning |
| *Buna ziua* | Good day |
| *Noapte buna* | Good night |
| *Ce mai faceti?* | How are you? |
| *Cum va numit?* | What's your name? |
| *Noroc!* | Good luck! |
| *Ce ořa este?* | What's the time? |
| *un, una* | one |
| *doi, doua* | two |
| *trei* | three |
| *patru* | four |
| *cinci* | five |
| *sase* | six |
| *sapte* | seven |
| *opt* | eight |
| *nouă* | nine |
| *zece* | ten |

**Famous People:**

Constantin Brâncuşi (1876–1957)
*Sculptor*

Nicolae Ceausescu (1918–1989)
*Dictator*

Nadia Comaneci (1961– )
*Olympic gymnast*

Alexandru Ioan Cuza (1820–1873)
*Prince of the United Principalities
of Moldavia and Walachia*

Mihai Eminescu (1850–1889)
*Poet*

Georges Enesco (1881–1955)
*Composer and violinist*

Marie (1875–1938)
*Queen*

Andrei Şaguna (1809–1873)
*Romanian Orthodox leader*

Vlad Ţepeş (1431–1476)
*Ruler of Walachia; basis for the fictional character Dracula*

Lászlo Tökes (1952– )
*Reformed Church pastor*

# To Find Out More

## Books

▶ Bachman, Ronald D., ed. *Romania: A Country Study*. Washington, D.C.: Federal Research Division, Library of Congress, 1991.

▶ Behr, Edward. *Kiss the Hand You Cannot Bite: The Rise and Fall of the Ceauşescus*. New York: Villard Books, 1991.

▶ Kovi, Paul. *Transylvanian Cuisine*. New York, Crown Publishers, Inc., 1985.

▶ Richardson, Dan and Tim Burford. *Romania: the Rough Guide*. London: The Rough Guides, 1995.

▶ Sanborne, Mark. *Nations in Transition: Romania*. New York: Facts on File, 1996.

▶ Sheehan, Sean. *Romania*. New York: Marshall Cavendish, 1994.

▶ Stewart, Gail B. *Romania*. New York: Crestwood House, 1991.

▶ Treptow, Kurt W., ed. *A History of Romania*. Iaşi, Romania: The Center for Romanian Studies, The Romanian Cultural Foundation, 1995.

## Websites

▶ **The Government of Romania**
http://domino.kappa.ro/guvern

▶ **Political Institutions in Romania**
http://www.presidency.ro/engleza

▶ **Romanian Art and Culture**
http://indis.ici.ro/romania/culture

# Index

Page numbers in *italics* indicate illustrations.

# Meet the Author

Terri Willis learned to love books when she was read to every day by her mother while growing up in Minnesota. "I've always loved to escape into books," she said. "Sometimes, when I was a kid, I'd be reading three or four of them at a time, and I always brought books and a flashlight under the covers with me at night."

Now, it's a thrill for her to be able to write books for a new generation of readers.

She begins researching her topic in her local library, checking out the information available there. Usually there's a lot in the reference collections and on the stacks. Encyclopedias are good starting points, too, she said, giving her a brief understanding of the topic.

From there, it becomes a matter of filling in the blanks— adding the detail that can make a book exciting and loaded with neat information. She hunts down materials from government agencies and other organizations, hits the Internet for up-to-minute facts, and sorts through the collections of

major libraries on university campuses and in large cities. "I love searching out the details," Terri said. "I especially like hanging out in big libraries. To me, it's like panning for gold. There's usually a lot to sift through, but occasionally you find that great nugget of a fact that really adds to the book."

Terri got her degree in journalism at the University of Wisconsin–Madison. She is the author of nine books for children and young adults, mostly on geography and the environment, including another Enchantment of the World book, *Libya*, and two for Children's Press Saving Planet Earth series. She's also written for a geography newsletter and several newspapers and magazines. She lives in Cedarburg, Wisconsin, with her husband, Harry, and their two young daughters, Andrea and Elizabeth, who are read to every day!

# Photo Credits